OTHER WORKS BY PRIMO LEVI

A TRANQUIL STAR

'Full of philosophical wit, pastiche and, at times, dark foreboding'
Daily Telegraph

'Exquisitely controlled intellectual explosions ... these stories
demonstrate that Levi never lost sight of the essential' *Sunday Times*

'Each story has a small kernel to it – a turn of phrase, a memory, a
fantastic invention, a strange meeting – which jolts or moves or raises
a smile ... these wry, witty and often mutedly moving stories are a
welcome addition to the canon of a remarkable writer' *Spectator*

'His writing brims with metaphorical reflection and a love of
storytelling' *Metro*

'Will perhaps begin to change our understanding of Levi'
Literary Review

'These stories fizz, perplex, illuminate and startle, like burning
sparklers on firework night' *Socialist Review*

'This is a beautiful and profound book' *Jewish Chronicle*

'Thoughtful, quirky and wry ... refreshingly understated and delicate'
New Statesman

PRIMO LEVI

A TRANQUIL STAR

Unpublished Stories

TRANSLATED BY ANN GOLDSTEIN
AND ALESSANDRA BASTAGLI

PENGUIN BOOKS

PENGUIN CLASSICS

Published by the Penguin Group
Penguin Books Ltd, 80 Strand, London WC2R 0RL, England
Penguin Group (USA) Inc., 375 Hudson Street, New York, New York 10014, USA
Penguin Group (Canada), 90 Eglinton Avenue East, Suite 700, Toronto, Ontario, Canada M4P 2Y3
(a division of Pearson Penguin Canada Inc.)
Penguin Ireland, 25 St Stephen's Green, Dublin 2, Ireland (a division of Penguin Books Ltd)
Penguin Group (Australia), 250 Camberwell Road, Camberwell, Victoria 3124, Australia
(a division of Pearson Australia Group Pty Ltd)
Penguin Books India Pvt Ltd, 11 Community Centre, Panchsheel Park, New Delhi – 110 017, India
Penguin Group (NZ), 67 Apollo Drive, Rosedale, North Shore 0632, New Zealand
(a division of Pearson New Zealand Ltd)
Penguin Books (South Africa) (Pty) Ltd, 24 Sturdee Avenue,
Rosebank, Johannesburg 2196, South Africa

Penguin Books Ltd, Registered Offices: 80 Strand, London WC2R 0RL, England

www.penguin.com

First published in the United States of America by W.W. Norton & Company, Inc.,
by arrangement with Giulio Einaudi Editore 2007
First published in Great Britain by Penguin Classics 2007
Published in Penguin Modern Classics 2008

1

Stories selected by Ann Goldstein
Copyright © W.W. Norton & Company, Inc., 2007
English translations copyright © Ann Goldstein and Alessandra Bastagli, 2007
English translation of "Censorship in Bitinia" copyright © Jenny McPhee, 2007

The moral rights of the translators and introducer have been asserted

English translations of the stories "Bear Meat" and "A Tranquil Star" first appeared in
The New Yorker.
English translations of the story "Knall" first appeared in *Harper's*.
The present edition includes short stories selected from the following works by Primo Levi:
Storie naturali, published in 1966; *Vizio di forma*, first published in 1971, second edition published
in 1987 with a letter from the author; *Lilìt*, published in 1981; *Pagine sparse 1946–1980* and
Pagine sparse 1981–1987, which first appeared in *Opere I* and *II*, published in 1997.

Storie naturali, *Vizio di forma*, and *Lilìt* are also collected in the volume *Tutti i racconti*,
edited by Marco Belpoliti, published in 2005.

Printed in England by Clays Ltd, St Ives plc

978-0-141-18891-1

Contents

CONTENTS

Editor's Introduction

Primo Levi is known to English readers mainly for his writings on the Holocaust—*Survival in Auschwitz* and *The Truce*—and for the autobiographical *Periodic Table*. Yet he was a prolific writer of stories and essays; he had, he once recalled, been writing poems and stories even before he was deported to Auschwitz in 1943. His first efforts when he returned to Turin included both poems and stories, in addition to what he was writing about his experiences in the concentration camp; and he continued to write stories until his sudden death, in 1987. This new book of stories, the first untranslated fiction of Levi's to be published in the United States since 1990,* is intended to introduce readers to a Primo Levi who may be somewhat unfamiliar to them.

* The only other new work to appear in the United States since 1990 is entitled *Auschwitz Report*, a book about the conditions in Auschwitz, which was written by Levi with Leonardo De Benedetti in 1946, and published here by Verso in 2006.

THE EARLIEST story in *A Tranquil Star*, "The Death of Marinese," dates from 1949, when Levi was virtually unknown as
a writer, and was first published in *Il Ponte*, a liberal-socialist
journal based in Florence that had published a chapter of *Survival in Auschwitz* two years earlier. It tells of a captured partisan who, as he is being transported in a truck to prison,
decides to set off the grenade in the belt of a German soldier
guarding him. In the space of a few pages, Levi re-creates the
suffocating sensation of capture, the feverish yet clear-headed
state of mind, the sharp hatred of the Germans, the weary
intensity of despair that lead to Marinese's act. The story may
have been based on an account that Levi had heard, but there
is at least a grain of personal experience. Levi had joined a
partisan group in the fall of 1943 and was almost immediately
captured himself; on the bus that was transporting him to
prison, he writes, in the chapter "Gold," in *The Periodic Table*,
he had the thought of pulling the cord on the grenade of a
German soldier with his back turned to him, but—unlike
Marinese—he didn't have the courage.

"Bear Meat," the second story here, was published in 1961
in *Il Mondo*, a political and literary journal based in Rome. It,
too, is a story about foolhardiness and courage, but utterly
different from "Marinese," in its expansive storytelling and
cast of characters, its complex format (the double narrator
and the story within a story), mountain setting, and overtly
moralistic tone. The mountains and mountain climbing
were important to Levi, and the story recapitulates some of
his own experiences. In a 1984 interview he said, "I began

going up into the mountains when I was thirteen or fourteen. In my family there was a tradition of seeing the mountains as a source of strength. . . . Not mountaineering as such, no climbing rockfaces. . . . You just went up into the mountains." Levi did not write other stories of this type, nor did he ever include this one in a collection, perhaps because of its singularity; however, the second part, the story of the character called Carlo, appears—with the character's actual name—in the "Iron" chapter of *The Periodic Table*.

"Censorship in Bitinia" was published the same year as "Bear Meat," in the same journal (and then in Levi's first Italian collection, *Storie Naturali*). Short and satirical, without characters, it makes a sharp contrast to "Bear Meat." Bitinia (a made-up country), Levi tells us, has a problem finding qualified people to do the work of censorship; one difficulty is the job hazards, which may include "various sensory system troubles," such as "exaggerated reactions to certain colors or flavors, which regularly develop, after remissions and relapses, into serious psychological anomalies and perversions." Levi describes the various solutions, keeping the slightly detached, almost deadpan tone of the reporter. The story seems to have been inspired by the Christian Democratic politician Mario Scelba, who served as Interior Minister and Prime Minister in the nineteen-fifties and was known for his rigid suppression of dissent, especially on the left.

The two remaining stories in Part I of this volume, "Knall" and "In the Park," were written between 1968 and 1970, and published in the Italian volume *Vizio di Forma*. In a letter to his publisher about the stories he was writing in the sixties, Levi says that he is trying to give form to a perception he has of "an unraveling in the world, a breach, large or small, a 'defect of form' that annihilates one or another aspect of our civilization or our moral universe." In the story "Knall," for example, he invents "a small, smooth cylinder, as long and thick as a Tuscan cigar, and not much heavier," which comes "solid-colored, gray or red" or "in wrappers printed with revoltingly tasteless little scenes and comic figures." The purpose of this harmless-sounding device (its popularity is compared to that of the hula hoop), presented as a sort of toy, is, it turns out, to kill. Yet the tone remains light and conversational, and the details are from ordinary life; for example, the idea that displaying a knall on one's person is "de rigueur" in certain circles, or that its use has spread without any help from the media.

"In the Park," on the other hand, creates an entire fantasy world, a National Park of literary characters. Like Dante and Virgil in Purgatory, and Aeneas guided by the Sybil through the Underworld, Antonio, a new arrival, and James, his guide, tour the park and its inhabitants, who include the creations of many of Levi's favorite authors: François Villon, Conrad, Melville, Rabelais, the Milanese dialogue poet Carlo Porta, and, of course, Dante. It is an eclectic crowd, reflecting the broad range of Levi's interests. As a child he was often ill and had to be tutored at home; with that, and his father's vast library, he was able to read far beyond the narrow classical curriculum followed by the schools. (In school, in fact, he was less interested in literature than in science.) Levi's descriptions of the various characters of "In the Park" ("all cordial people, or at least varied and interesting") give him an opportunity for brief, often oblique, and humorous commentaries on literature and on human behavior in general.

IN CONTRAST to Part I, most of the stories in Part II were written in the late seventies and the eighties, after Levi had retired as director of the SIVA paint factory to become a full-time writer; before that, he had been able to write only at night and on weekends. As he told Philip Roth in an interview in 1986, "I worked in a factory for nearly thirty years and I must admit that there is no incompatibility between being a chemist and being a writer: in fact, there is a mutual reinforcement. But factory life, and particularly factory managing—to direct a factory involves many other matters, far from chemistry. . . . Consequently I truly felt that I had been 'born again' when I reached retirement age and could resign." That was in 1975, the year *The Periodic Table* came out, cementing Levi's reputation in Italy. In the next decade, he published *The Wrench* (1978), *If Not Now, When?* (1982), *Other People's Trades* (1985), and *The Drowned and the Saved* (1986), and became a regular contributor to the Turin newspaper *La Stampa*, for which he had written sporadically since 1959. It was not until 1984, when *The Periodic Table* appeared in English, that Levi gained recognition, and acclaim, in America.

Seven of the twelve stories in this section are from *Lilith*, a three-part collection published in Italy in 1981. The first part of *Lilith*—which appeared in English as *Moments of Reprieve*—is entitled *Passato Prossimo* (*Simple Past*), and the stories take up the theme of the Holocaust. The two other parts, which have not appeared before in English, are entitled *Futuro Anteriore* (*Future Perfect*) and *Presente Indicativo* (*Present Indicative*). The stories taken from *Future Perfect*—"A Tranquil Star," "The Gladiators," "The Fugitive," and "The Magic Paint"—are in the gentle fantasy vein. Those from *Present Indicative*—"The Sorcerers," "The Molecule's Defiance," and "The Girl in the Book"—are, as the rubric indicates, closer to everyday life, and, Levi wrote, "indicative of our time."

In "The Gladiators," published in the magazine *L'Automobile*, modern-day gladiator-athletes enter the stadium to go up against cars. "The Magic Paint," which appeared in *Il Mondo* in 1973, is about the search for a paint that wards off evil. In just a few pages we learn how a paint sample is analyzed, and the dangers of trying to escape our fate, moving from the practical analysis to the scientific explication of the properties of the element tantalum and finally to the disastrous experiment with the glasses of the narrator's old friend. "The Molecule's Defiance," like "The Magic Paint," takes place in a paint factory, but, unlike "The Magic Paint," with its layer of the supernatural, sticks to real life, to the science of making a varnish and what can go wrong in the process.

Of the five other stories in Part II, four—"One Night," "Bureau of Vital Statistics," "Buffet Dinner," and "Fra Diavolo on the Po"—were first published in *La Stampa* and were not collected in Levi's lifetime, while the fifth, "The TV Fans from Delta Cep.," was first published in *L'Astronomia*. "One Night" is perhaps the eeriest of the stories here, the only one that lacks an underlying humor and seems to speak of pure destruction. It's not specifically about the Holocaust, yet one can almost not help but think of the death camps as the story opens with a train in a landscape that may seem beautiful but that turns out to harbor devastation.

Levi often wrote about animals. He was interested in biology before he decided to become a chemist; when he was fifteen, his father gave him a microscope and his first explorations were of the insect and animal world. This passion for detail can be seen in his writing about animals, and he is a close observer of both physical characteristics and behavior. In "Buffet Dinner" the reader is not told right away that the protagonist is a kangaroo; in fact, although a tail is mentioned on the first page, and other facts accumulate, the species isn't named until more than halfway through the story. In "The TV Fans from Delta Cep." is also a creature, of a sort, but an invented one. (The story is presented as a transmission from the inhabitants of a distant planet to Piero Bianucci, the editor of *La Stampa* and the host of a popular science show on TV; this transmission has been "translated by Primo Levi.")

The final story in this volume, the highly lyrical "A Tranquil Star" (published not only in *La Stampa* but in the journal *L'Astronomia*), begins with a discussion of language and the difficulties, and the importance, of being rigorous, scrupulous, and exacting with words ("how many times as high as a high tower is a very high tower?"). Levi's ability to do so is one of the harrowing strengths of his writing about the Holocaust, and the language of his stories, whatever the subject—the mountain landscape, the invented knall, the process of making a paint—is similarly compelling, if on a smaller scale. The description of how atoms bond in "The Molecule's Defiance" is a marvel of simple language and complex science. While Levi sometimes does use a technical or scientific term—the "adiabatic observatory" ("Delta Cep."); "gelatinization" and "premature polymerization" ("The Molecule's Defiance"); "diplopia" ("Censorship in Bitinia")—it is always as part of the careful construction of the moment that the particular story presents.

"I HOPE that each story properly fulfills its task, which is only that of condensing into a few pages, and conveying to the reader, a particular memory, a state of mind, or even just a thought. Some are happy and some sad, because our days are happy and sad." Levi was here speaking of the stories in *Lilith*, but certainly what he says could apply to all his short pieces. "In my opinion," he wrote, "a story has as many meanings as there are keys in which it can be read, and so all interpretations are true, in fact the more interpretations a story can give, the more ambiguous it is. I insist on this word, 'ambiguous': a story must be ambiguous or else it is a news story, therefore everything is valid, rationality is valid, the science-fiction world is valid, and even the sensation of dreams is valid." For the reader who knows Levi's other works, these stories are a treasure; for the reader who does not, or who knows only the Holocaust works, they are a revelation, a chance to spend time with a precise, imaginative, and surprising companion.

ANN GOLDSTEIN
New York, September 2006

TRANSLATION CREDITS

The following stories have been translated by Ann Goldstein:

Knall
In the Park
The Magic Paint
Gladiators
The Fugitive
The Sorcerers
The Girl in the Book
The Molecule's Defiance
A Tranquil Star

The following stories have been translated by Alessandra Bastagli:

The Death of Marinese
Bear Meat
One Night
Fra Diavolo on the Po
Bureau of Vital Statistics
Buffet Dinner
The TV Fans from Delta Cep.

The following story has been translated by Jenny McPhee:

Censorship in Bitinia

Acknowledgments

The stories that appear in this volume were published in Italian in 1997 in two volumes edited by Marco Belpoliti. We would like to thank both him and the entire editorial staff at Giulio Einaudi Editore for putting together Primo Levi's *Opere*, which is now being prepared for English publication. We would also like to thank Robert Weil, at Norton, for conceiving of this separate project and making it possible. Thanks also to Francesco Bastagli for his invaluable guidance and close reading of the translation against the original text and to Nunzia and Daniela Rondanini and Valentina Germani for assisting with the dialect.

Ann Goldstein
Alessandra Bastagli

PART I

EARLY
STORIES

The Death of Marinese

No one was killed. Sante and Marinese were the only ones captured by the Germans. It made no sense, it was almost incredible, that, of us all, the two of them had been taken. But the older men in the group knew that it is always those who are captured of whom it is later said "Who would have guessed!" And they also knew why.

When the two were taken away, the sky was gray and the road was covered with snow that had hardened into ice. The truck barreled downhill with the engine off: the chains on the wheels rattled around the bends and clanked rhythmically along the straight stretches. About thirty Germans were standing in the back of the truck, packed shoulder to shoulder, some of them hanging onto the frame of the canvas roof. The tarp had come loose, so that a thin sleet struck their faces and came to rest on the fabric of their uniforms.

Sante was wounded; he sat mute and still on the rear bench of the truck, while Marinese was at the front, standing, with his back against the driver's cab. Trembling with fever, Marinese felt himself slowly overcome by a growing drowsiness, so that, taking advantage of a bump in the road, he slid to the wet floor and remained sitting there, an inanimate object amid the muddy boots, his bare head wedged between the bony hips of two soldiers.

The pursuit had been long and exhausting, and he wanted nothing more than this—for it all to be over, to remain sitting, to have no more decisions to make, to surrender to the heat of his fever and rest. He knew that he would be interrogated, probably beaten, and then almost certainly killed, and he knew, too, that soon all this would regain importance. But for now he felt strangely protected by a burning shield of fever and sleep, as if it were an insulation of cotton wool that separated him from the rest of the world, from the facts of the day and the things to come. Vacation, he thought, almost in a dream: how long had it been since he had had a vacation?

With his eyes closed, he felt as if he were submerged in a long, narrow tunnel that had been dug into a soft, tepid substance, crimson like the light that penetrates closed eyelids. His feet and his head were cold, and he seemed to be moving with difficulty, as if pushed, toward the exit, which was far away, but which he would finally, inexorably, reach. The exit was barred by a swirl of snow and a tangle of hard, frozen metal.

For Marinese a long time passed in this way, during which

he made no attempt to break out of his cradle of fever. The truck reached the plain, and the Germans stopped to take off the chains. Then the drive resumed—faster, the jolts more violent.

Perhaps nothing would have happened if the Germans hadn't suddenly begun to sing. A voice, starting up in the cab, reached them muffled and indistinct. But once the first verse was over, a second burst forth like thunder from every chest, drowning out the rumble of the engine and the rush of the wind—even Marinese's fever was overwhelmed. He found himself again able to act and therefore, in some way, obliged to take action—which was how it was for all of us at that time.

The song was long; every verse ended abruptly, in the German manner, and the soldiers stamped twice on the wooden floor with their hobnailed boots. Marinese had opened his eyes and raised his head again, and every time they stamped their feet he perceived a light touch on his shoulder: he soon realized that it was the handle of a grenade, tucked diagonally into the belt of the man on his left. In that moment the idea took hold.

It's probable that, at least in the beginning, he hadn't considered using the grenade to save himself, to open up a path with his own hands, even though, as we shall see, his final actions cannot be interpreted otherwise. It's more likely that he was moved by hatred and rancor (feelings that had become habitual to us by then, almost an elementary reflex) toward those blond men in green, well nourished and well armed, who for many months had forced us to live in hiding. Perhaps more than that, he wanted to take revenge and yet at the same time cleanse himself of the shame of a final escape—the shame that weighed and still weighs on our souls. In fact, Marinese had a gentle soul, and none of us thought him capable of killing, except in self-defense, revenge, or anger.

Without turning his head, Marinese carefully groped for the handle of the grenade (the type shaped like a stick, with a timer) and, bit by bit, he unscrewed the safety cap, using the jolts of the vehicle to conceal his movements. This operation was easy enough, but Marinese never would have thought that it would be so difficult to occupy and get through the last ten seconds of his life—he would have to fight hard, with all his will and with all his physical strength, so that everything would go according to plan. He dedicated his last few moments to this alone: not to self-pity, not to the thought of God, not to taking leave of the memory of those he loved.

With the cord firmly in his grasp, Marinese tried to imagine, in an orderly fashion, what would happen in the ten seconds between the rip and the explosion. The Germans might not notice, might simply register his sudden movement, or might understand everything. The first option was the most favorable: the ten seconds would be his own, his time, to spend as he wished, perhaps to think of home, perhaps to think of how he would manage, taking shelter at the last minute behind the man on his right, but then he would have to count to ten and that thought was strangely worrisome. "Fool," he thought suddenly. "Here I am racking my brains with the cord in my hand. I could have thought of it sooner, couldn't I. Now the first son of a bitch who sees the cap missing . . . But no, I can always pull, no matter what happens." He laughed to himself: "(Even a situation like this has its advantages!) Even if they hit me in the back of the neck? Even if they shoot me?" . . . But yes, thanks to some mental mechanism, evidently illusory and distorted by the imminence of the decision, Marinese felt sure he could pull the cord no matter what, even the very instant he lost consciousness, perhaps even the instant after.

But unexpectedly, out of some unexplored depths, from some recess of his body—the animal, rebel body that has trouble deciding to die—something was born and grew beyond measure, something dark and primeval, and unfathomable, because its growth arrests and then replaces all the powers of knowledge and determination. It dawned on Marinese that this was fear, and he understood that, in a moment, it would be too late. He filled his lungs to prepare for battle and pulled the cord with all his might.

Rage was unleashed. A paw struck his shoulder, followed by an avalanche of bodies. But Marinese was able to tear the bomb away from the belt and roll up like a hedgehog, face down, his knees drawn up against his chest, the grenade wedged between his knees, his arms tight around them. The fierce blows of fists, musket butts, and heels rained down on his back; hard hands tried to violate the stronghold of his contracted limbs. But all in vain: it was not enough to overcome the insensitivity to pain and the primordial strength that, for just a few moments, nature grants us in a time of dire need.

For three or four seconds Marinese lay under a pile of bodies writhing in violent battle, every fiber of his being contracted. Then he heard the squeal of the brakes, the truck stopping, and the rushed thuds of men jumping to the ground. At that instant he sensed that the time had come. In a final, perhaps involuntary extension of all his powers, he tried, too late, to free himself of the grenade.

The explosion ripped apart the bodies of four Germans, and his own. Sante was executed by the Germans on the spot. The truck was abandoned, and we captured it the following night.

Bear Meat

Evenings spent in a mountain hut are among the most sublime and intense that life holds. I mean a real hut, the kind where you seek shelter after a four-, five-, or six-hour climb and where you find few so-called comforts.

Not that chairlifts and cable cars and such comforts are to be looked down on: they are, on the contrary, logical achievements of our society, which is what it is, and must be either accepted or rejected in its totality—and those who are able to reject it are few. But the advent of the chairlift puts an end to a valuable process of natural selection, by which those who reach the hut are sure to find, in its pure state, a small sample of a little-known human subspecies.

Its members are people who don't speak much and of whom others don't speak at all, so there is no mention of them in the literature of most countries, and they should not be confused with other, vaguely similar types, who do speak, and of whom others speak: hot shots, extreme climbers, members of famous international expeditions, professionals, etc. All worthy people, but this story is not about them.

I ARRIVED at the hut at sunset, and I was very tired. I stayed outside, on the wooden porch, to consider the frozen mystery of the seracs at my feet until everything had vanished behind silent ghosts of fog, and then I went in.

Inside it was almost dark. By the glow of a small carbide lamp one could distinguish a dozen human figures gathered around three or four tables. I sat down at a table and opened my backpack. Across from me was a tall, large man, middle-aged, with whom I exchanged a few words about the weather and our plans for the following day. This is a standard conversation, like the classic opening moves of a chess game, where what matters, much more than what one says (which is brief and obvious), is the tone in which one says it.

We found ourselves in agreement on the fact that the weather was uncertain (it always is in the mountains; when it isn't, it is nonetheless declared to be so, for obvious magical reasons), and on the forecast for the following day. A little later, two lanky men in their twenties entered, with long beards and ravenous eyes. They had arrived from another valley and were attempting an intricate series of crossings. They sat down at our table.

After we had eaten, we started to drink. Wine is a more complex substance than one might think, and, above two thousand meters, and at close to zero degrees centigrade, it displays interesting behavioral anomalies. It changes flavor, loses the bite of alcohol, and regains the mildness of the grape from which it comes. One can take it in heavy doses without any undesired effects. In fact, it eliminates fatigue, loosens and warms the limbs, and leads to a fanciful mood. It is no longer a luxury or a vice but a metabolic necessity, like water on the plains. It is a well-known fact that vines grow better on a slope: could there be a connection?

Once we started drinking, the conversation at our table became much less impersonal. Each of us spoke of our initiation, and we established with some surprise that we had all begun our mountaineering careers with an extremely foolish act.

As it turned out, the best of these foolish acts, and the best told, was the one recounted by the tall, large man.

"I was fifteen. A friend of mine, Saverio, was also fifteen. Another, Luigi, was seventeen. We had gone out a number of times together, to fifteen hundred, two thousand meters, without a plan or a destination; I should say, without a conscious destination, but, in essence, impelled by a subtle desire to get ourselves in trouble and then get ourselves out of it. Nothing easier: it's enough to go straight up the mountain following your nose, in any direction, by the steepest slope, then struggle for a quarter of an hour across the mountain-side, and then try to get back down. Of course, one also learns a few things in this process: that pine trees, when they're available, make safe and friendly supports, especially during the descent, and that scree is hard to climb but easy to descend by. One learns different types of grasses, those peculiar terraced slopes, and the art of losing the trail and finding it again. Above all, one learns the limits, both quan-titative and qualitative, of one's own strength: when the breath, the legs, and the heart give out, and when, so to speak, it's psychosomatic. It's a great school—I wish I had attended it longer.

"September came and we felt like lions. Luigi said, 'The G. Pass is twenty-four hundred meters high—eleven hun-dred vertical meters from here. According to the guide-books, it should be a three-hour climb, but it'll take us barely two. There's nothing difficult, just scree and small rocks—no snow this time of year. On the other side, there's a six-hundred-meter descent, one hour, and we arrive at the border-patrol hut; you can see it clearly here on the map. Then an easy return along the road. We'll leave at two today; at four we're at the top, at five at the hut, and home in time for dinner.'

"That was Luigi. We met at his house at two, with our good boots on our feet, but no backpacks, no rope (about whose use none of us had any real notion anyway; but we knew—having studied the Alpine Club guidebook—the theory of the double rope, the respective merits of hemp and manila, the technique for rescuing someone from a crevasse, and other fine points), a hundred grams of chocolate in our pockets, and (may God forgive us!) wearing shorts.

"We progressed well uphill. First, through a pine forest, spurning the mule trail and the shortcuts, and sampling the blueberries; then through an alluvial cone, wasting precious energy. It was the first time we had set off without grownups getting on our nerves with their advice, without uncles, without experts. We were drunk on our freedom, and because of this we delighted in the dirtiest high-school slang, accompanied with lofty quotations from the classics, for example:

> "It is another path that you must take . . .
> if you would leave this savage wilderness";

Or:

> That was no path for those with cloaks of lead;
> for he and I—he, light; I, with support—
> could hardly make it up from spur to spur.

And also:

> . . . he'd see another spur,
> saying: "That is the one you will grip next,
> but try it first to see if it is firm."

"Forgive me if I get a little carried away. You see, I'm not a Dante expert, and yet, believe me, one of these days an honest man will come along and prove that Dante couldn't have just invented these founding principles of rock climbing—he must have been here or in a similar place. And when he says:

> Remember, reader, if you've ever been
> caught in the mountains by a mist through which
> you only saw as moles see through their skin—

I congratulate him! I, for one, never doubted that he was a professional.

"At any rate, we were climbing at a brisk pace, saying and doing foolish things. And so it happened that we reached the pass at six, not at four, near collapse, and with a certain trembling in our knees that wasn't just from exhaustion. Saverio was the worst off. Luigi and I were already at the top and saw him struggling among the loose rocks fifty meters below us. "'Now you must cast aside your laziness!'" Luigi had the gall to shout to him. At which the poor boy paused to catch his breath, looked upward like Christ on the Cross, then clambered up to us and breathed out, in a faint voice, the implausible yet utterly correct reply: "'Go on, for I am strong and confident.'"

"When all three of us were at the pass, two unhappy truths became clear. One, that night was falling; and I swear on this bottle that I have never since then (and many years have passed) seen darkness fall in the mountains without feeling an emptiness here in the pit of my stomach. The other truth was that we were trapped.

"From the pass, there was no logical descent to the hut.

There was a gentle, rocky valley, with no human trace, and beyond it a terrifying precipice, not vertical, no, but of broken rock and gullies of crumbling earth—one of those places no one ever wants to go because you'll break your neck without glory or satisfaction.

"With the last light, we pushed on all the way to the edge: you could see the big dark leap of the valley and, if you stuck your nose out, even the light in the hut, almost beneath you. But as for getting down there on our own, we couldn't even consider it; we sat there and started shouting. We took turns. Saverio shouted and prayed. Luigi shouted and cursed. I just shouted. We shouted until we were hoarse.

"Toward midnight, the light in the hut split into two lights, and one of the two blinked three times. It was a signal: we shouted three times in response. At that, a faraway voice called, 'We're coming,' and we replied with a cacophony of shouts. The voice asked, 'Where are you?,' and we three, without a single match among us, blurted out confused and irrelevant information, all at the same time.

"Our rescuers, poor devils, cursed as they climbed, and stopped now and then to sing, drink, and laugh loudly. They weren't very enthusiastic. Many years later, I also happened to be part of a rescue party, so I know exactly how they felt. These expeditions are tedious and dangerous affairs, and in most cases they can only lead to trouble, because no one wants to pay for the emergency supplies—least of all the rescued, who are rarely solvent.

"They reached us at around two in the morning; and here

I must tell you that, on top of everything else, they were members of the border patrol. Once they'd found us, a signal was sent to the valley with a flashlight. 'Who are they?' a voice asked from below. 'It's just three whiny *gagnô*' was the fierce reply, in dialect. Then, turning to us, 'Is this what they teach you in school?'

"After that, they tied us up like salami and lowered us down to the valley without talking to us but stopping often to drink, and curse, and guffaw among themselves. 'Pass me the bottle, please.'"

"I passed him the bottle and asked him what a *gagnô* was."

"'*Gagnô*,'" he said, "'means child, but it's a word loaded with mockery. Second-grade kids say it to first graders.'

"That's how I started. It's not a story to be proud of, you might say. And I'm not. But I'm sure that even this foolish adventure was useful to me later. These are things that make your back broad, which isn't something Nature gives everyone. I read somewhere—and the person who wrote this was not a mountaineer but a sailor—that the sea's only gifts are harsh blows and, occasionally, the opportunity to feel strong. Now, I don't know much about the sea, but I do know that that's the way it is here. And I also know how important it is in life not necessarily to be strong but to feel strong, to measure yourself at least once, to find yourself at least once in the most ancient of human conditions, facing blind, deaf stone alone, with nothing to help you but your own hands and your own head. . . . But, excuse me, that's another story. The one I told you ends like this. They called me 'whiny *gagnô'* for years. Some people still do and, I assure you, I don't mind at all."

He drank and silently busied himself with the complex rituals of a pipe smoker.

"I, TOO, started with an extremely foolish act," a voice interjected at this point, and then we noticed that there were no longer four of us but five at the table. The voice had come from a man who, in the dim light, appeared to be thin, balding at the temples, with a sharp face furrowed by shifting wrinkles. He told his story at an uneven pace, swallowing his words and leaving sentences incomplete, as if his tongue had difficulty following the thread of his thoughts; at other times he struggled to find the words and would stop as if under a spell.

"There were three of us, too, but not so young—in our twenties. One was Antonio, and I wouldn't want to say much about him, nor would I know how to. He was a fine, handsome youth, smart, sensitive, tenacious, and bold, but with something in him that was elusive, dark, wild. We were at that age when you have the need and the instinct and the immodesty to inflict on others everything that is seething in your head and elsewhere; it's an age that can last a long time, but ends at the first compromise. Yet with him, even at that age, nothing had slipped out of his wrapping of restraint; nothing escaped from his inner world—though we sensed it to be rich and dense—except some rare allusion dramatically cut short. He

Primo Levi

was like a cat, if I may put it this way, whom you live with for years but who never allows you to get under his sacred skin.

"The third was Carlo, our leader. He is dead; it's best to say it right away, because one can't help speaking in a different way of the dead than of the living. He died in a way that suited him, not in the mountains, but the way one dies in the mountains. Doing what he had to do: not the kind of duty imposed by someone else, or by the state, but the kind that one chooses for oneself. He would have put it differently, called it 'reaching the end of the line,' for example, because he didn't like big words, or, for that matter, words.

"He was the kind of boy who doesn't study for seven months, who is known as a rebel and a dunce, and then in the eighth month he absorbs all the courses as if they were water and comes through with straight A's. He spent the summer as a shepherd—not a shepherd of souls, no, a shepherd of sheep, and not to show off or to be eccentric but happily, for love of the earth and the grass. And in the winter, whenever he got restless, he would tie his skis to his bicycle and 'go up' alone, with no money, only an artichoke in one pocket and the other full of salad. He would come back in the evening or maybe the following day, having slept who knows where, and the more storms and hunger he had endured, the happier and healthier he was. When I met him, he already had a considerable mountaineering career behind him, while I was still a novice. But he was reluctant to talk about it: he wasn't the type—which I respect, because I'm like that, too—who goes into the mountains to be able to tell a story. On the other hand, it was as if no one had taught him how to speak, just as no one had taught him how to ski: because he spoke the way nobody speaks, he voiced only the essence of things.

"He seemed to be made of steel. If necessary, he could carry a backpack that weighed thirty kilos as if it were nothing, but usually he traveled without a pack: his pockets were enough. Besides the vegetables, they held a piece of bread, a pocketknife, sometimes the Alpine Club guidebook, and always a spool of wire for emergency repairs. He could walk for two days without eating, or eat three meals in one sitting and then be off. Once, I saw him at three thousand meters in February, in the sleet, bare-chested, eating calmly, a spectacle so upsetting to two men nearby that it turned their stomachs. I have a picture at home of the whole scene."

He paused, as if to catch his breath. People from the other tables had gone to bed: in the sudden silence we distinctly heard the deep roar of a serac, like the bones of a giant trying in vain to turn over in his bed of rock.

"I beg your pardon. I'm no longer young, and I know that it's a desperate endeavor to clothe a man in words. This one in particular. A man like this, when he's dead, is dead forever. He's not the kind you tell stories about or build monuments to; he's all in his actions, and, once those are over, nothing remains—nothing but, precisely, words. So, every time I try to talk about him, to bring him back to life, as I'm doing now, I feel a great sadness, an emptiness, as if I were on a cliff, and I have to be silent, or else drink."

He was silent, drank, and continued.

"So one Saturday morning in February Carlo came to us. 'Tomorrow, eh?' he said. In his language, what he meant was that, since the weather was good, we could leave the next day for the winter ascent of the Tooth of M., which we had been planning for a while.

"I won't give you all the technical details. I'll tell you, briefly, that we left the following morning, not too early (Carlo didn't like watches—he felt their tacit, continuous warning as an arbitrary intrusion); that we plunged boldly into the fog; that we came out the other side at around one in the afternoon, the sun was shining, and we were on the ridge of the wrong mountain.

"Antonio said that we could go down a hundred meters or so, cross along the mountainside, and climb back up the next mountain. I, who was the most cautious and the least able, said that, while we were at it, we could just as well continue along the ridge and arrive at a different peak—it was only forty meters lower than the other one anyway—and be satisfied with that. Carlo, in perfect bad faith, said with a few harsh, cackling syllables that my proposal was fine but, then again, 'by the easy northwest ridge' we could reach the Tooth of M. in half an hour; and that it wasn't worth being twenty-one if you didn't allow yourself the luxury of taking the wrong path.

"'The easy northwest ridge' was described rock by rock in the battered guidebook that Carlo carried in his pocket, along with the wire I mentioned. He took this guidebook along not because he believed in it but for the exact opposite reason. He rejected it because he perceived it, too, as a constraint, and not just any constraint but a bastard creature, a detestable hybrid of snow and rock and paper. He took it with him into the mountains to scorn it, delighted if he could catch it in error, even if that error was to his own detriment and that of his climbing companions.

"The easy northwest ridge was truly easy, in fact elementary, in the summer, but the conditions we found that day were difficult. The rocks were wet on the side that faced the sun and glazed with ice on the side in the shade; between one rock spike and the next were pockets of wet snow where we sank up to our shoulders. We arrived at the right peak at five, two of us dragging ourselves pitifully, while Carlo was seized by a sinister hilarity that I found slightly irritating.

"'How will we get down?'

"'We'll figure it out,' Carlo said, and added mysteriously, 'The worst thing that happens is we taste bear meat.'

"Well, we tasted it, bear meat, in abundance, during the course of that night, the longest of my climbing career. It took us two hours to descend, feebly assisted by the rope. I'm sure you know what an infernal instrument a frozen rope is: ours had become a stiff, evil tangle that got caught on all the outcrops and clanged against the rock like a steel cable. At seven, we reached the shore of a small frozen lake. It was dark.

"We ate the little we had left, built a useless wall of stones to shelter us from the wind, and lay down on the ground to sleep, huddled side by side. We took turns—the man in the middle slept while the others acted as a buffer. For some reason I can't explain, our watches had stopped—perhaps because we had forgotten to wind them—and without watches we felt as if time, too, had frozen. We stood up now and then to get our circulation going, and it was always the same: the wind was always blowing, there was always a semblance of moon, always in the same spot in the sky, and in front of the moon a fantastic cavalcade of ragged clouds, always the same. We had taken off our shoes, and put our feet in our backpacks. At the first ghostly light, which seemed to radiate not from the sky but from the snow, we got up, our limbs numb and our eyes glazed from sleeplessness, hunger, and darkness, and found our shoes so frozen that, when struck, they rang like bells. In order to put them on we had to sit on them for half an hour, as if we were hatching eggs.

"But we returned to the valley on our own: and when the innkeeper asked us, chuckling, how it had gone, all the while stealing glances at our two-day stubble, we answered without hesitation that it had been a great outing, paid the bill, and left without losing our composure.

"That was bear meat. Now, you must believe me, gentlemen, many years have passed, and I regret having eaten so little of it. I think and hope that each of you has gleaned from life what I have—a certain measure of ease, respect, love, and success. Well, I'll tell you the truth, none of these things, not even remotely, has the taste of bear meat: the taste of being strong and free, which means free to make mistakes; the taste of feeling young in the mountains, of being your own master, which means master of the world.

"And, trust me, I am grateful to Carlo for having deliberately got us into trouble, for the night he made us spend, and for the various enterprises, senseless only on the surface, that he involved us in later on, and then for various others, not in the mountains, which I got into on my own, by following his doctrine. He was a young man full of earthly vigor who had a wisdom of his own, and may the earth in which he rests, not far from here, lie light on his bones, and bring the news, each year, of the return of the sun and of the frost."

THE SECOND narrator fell silent, and he seemed to me to be looking with some embarrassment toward the two young men, as if afraid that he had disturbed or offended them; then he filled his glass but did not drink. His last words had roused in me a rare echo, as if I had heard them somewhere before. And, in fact, I found almost those exact words in a book that is dear to me, by the same sailor, cited by the first man, who had written of the gifts of the sea.

Censorship in Bitinia

I have already mentioned elsewhere the drab cultural life of this country, which is based, to this day, on a system of patronage and entrusted to the interests of the wealthy or even just to professionals and artists, specialists and technicians, who are quite well paid.

Of particular interest is the solution that was proposed for—or, to be more precise, that spontaneously imposed itself upon—the problem of censorship. For various reasons, toward the end of the last decade there was a lively increase in the "need" for censorship in Bitinia; in just a few years, the existing central offices had to double their staff and establish local branches in almost all the provincial capitals. Difficulties were encountered, however, in recruiting the necessary personnel: first, because the work of a censor is, as is well known, arduous and subtle, requiring specialized training that even otherwise highly qualified people lack; and, second, because, according to recent statistics, the actual practice of censorship can be dangerous.

I do not mean to allude here to the immediate risk of retaliation, which the efficient Bitinese police have reduced almost to nil. This is something different: careful medical studies conducted in the workplace have brought to light a specific type of professional hazard, irksome in nature and apparently irreversible, called by its discoverer "paroxysmal dysthymia," or "Gowelius's disease." The initial clinical picture is vague and ill defined; then, as the years pass, various sensory-system troubles appear (diplopia, olfactory and auditory disorders, exaggerated reactions to, for example, certain colors or flavors), which regularly develop, after remissions and relapses, into serious psychological anomalies and perversions.

Consequently, and despite offers of high wages, the number of applicants for these government jobs rapidly decreased, and the workload of the existing career functionaries increased accordingly, until it rose to unprecedented levels. In the censorship offices, work pending (screenplays, scores, manuscripts, illustrated works, advertising posters) accumulated in such huge proportions that not only were the assigned storage spaces chockablock with documents but so were lobbies, corridors, and bathrooms as well. One case was reported of a division manager who, after an avalanche of files fell on him, died of suffocation before help arrived.

At first, mechanization provided a solution. Each branch was equipped with modern electronic systems: since I have only a basic knowledge of such things I am unable to describe with any precision how they worked, but I was told that their magnetic memory contained three distinct lists of words, *hints*, *plots*, *topics*,★ and frames of reference. Anything that corresponded to the first list was automatically deleted from the work under examination; anything on the second led to elimination of the entire work; anything on the third meant the immediate arrest and death by hanging of the author and the publisher.

The results were optimum with regard to processing the amount of work (in a few days the storage spaces in the offices were cleared), but in terms of quality they proved inadequate. There were outrageous cases of oversight: *Diary of a Sparrow*, by Claire Efrem, was "approved" and published, and it sold with incredible success, and yet the book was of dubious literary merit and patently immoral, the author having used blatantly transparent techniques to disguise through allusion and paraphrase all the most offensive aspects of today's ethics. Conversely, witness the sad case of Tuttle: Colonel Tuttle, the acclaimed critic and military historian, was forced to climb the gallows because in one of his volumes on the Caucasus campaign, owing to a simple mistake, the word "brigadier" appeared in altered form as "brassiere" and was recognized by the office of mechanized censorship in Issarvan as an obscene reference. The author of a modest manual on animal husbandry miraculously escaped the same tragic fate

★ In English in original.

because he had the means to flee abroad, whence he petitioned the Consulate before the court was able to pass sentence.

To these three episodes, which came to public attention, must be added numerous others, rumors of which spread by word of mouth but which were ignored by the officials because (as is obvious) any information about them fell, in its turn, under the censor's knife. A crisis situation erupted, resulting in a near total defection of the country's cultural forces: a situation that, despite a few feeble attempts at reversal, persists today.

There is, however, recent news that gives rise to some hope. A physiologist, whose name is being withheld, concluded one of his in-depth studies by revealing in a much discussed paper some new facets of the psychology of domestic animals. If pets are subjected to particular conditioning, they can not only learn simple jobs involving transport and organization but also make actual decisions.

Without a doubt, this is a vast and fascinating field, offering practically unlimited possibilities: to summarize what has been published in the Bitinese press up to the time of this writing, the work of censorship, which is damaging to the human brain, and is performed in far too rigid a manner by machines, could be profitably entrusted to animals trained for the purpose. Seriously considered, this disconcerting idea is not in itself absurd: in the last analysis, it is only a matter of decisions.

Curiously, the mammals closest to humans were found to be least useful for the task. Dogs, monkeys, and horses who underwent the conditioning proved to be poor judges precisely because they were too intelligent and sensitive. According to our anonymous scholar, they act far too passionately; they respond in unpredictable ways to the slightest foreign stimuli, which are inevitable in every workplace; they exhibit strange preferences, perhaps congenital but still inexplicable, for certain mental categories; and their own memories are uncontrollable and excessive. In sum, they reveal in these circumstances an *esprit de finesse* that would be detrimental to the goals of censorship.

Surprising results, on the other hand, were obtained with the common barnyard chicken: this animal's success is such that, as is common knowledge, four experimental offices have already been entrusted to teams of hens, under the control and supervision of experienced functionaries, naturally. The hens, besides being easily procured and costing little, both as an initial investment and for their subsequent maintenance, are capable of making rapid and definitive decisions. They stick scrupulously to the prescribed mental programs, and, given their cold, calm nature and their evanescent memory, they are not subject to distractions.

The general opinion around here is that in a few years the method will be extended to all the censorship offices in the country.

Approved by the censor.

Knall

It's not the first time something like this has happened here: a habit, or an object, or an idea becomes, within a few weeks, almost universally widespread, without the newspapers or the mass media having anything to do with it. There was the craze for the yo-yo, then for Chinese mushrooms, then Pop art, Zen Buddhism, the hula-hoop. Now it is time for the knall.

No one knows who invented it, but, to judge from the price (a four-inch knall costs the equivalent of 3,000 lire or a little more), it doesn't contain much in the way of costly materials or inventive genius or *software*.★ I bought one myself, down at the port, right in front of a cop, who didn't bat an eyelash. Of course I have no intention of using it. I just

★ In English in the original.

wanted to see how it works and how it's constructed: it seems a legitimate curiosity.

A knall is a small, smooth cylinder, as long and thick as a Tuscan cigar, and not much heavier: it is sold loose or in boxes of twenty. Some are solid-colored, gray or red, but the majority come in wrappers printed with revoltingly tasteless little scenes and comic figures, in the style of decorations on jukeboxes and pinball machines: a bare-breasted girl fires a knall at her suitor's enormous rear end; a pair of tiny Max and Moritz★ types with insolent expressions, chased by a furious farmer, turn at the last minute, knalls in hand, and the pursuer falls backward, kicking his long, booted legs in the air.

Nothing is known about the mechanism by which the knall kills, or at least nothing about it has been published to date. *Knall*, in German, means crack, bang, crash; *abknallen*, in the slang of the Second World War, came to mean "kill with a firearm," whereas the firing of a knall is typically silent. Maybe the name—unless it has a completely different origin, or is an abbreviation—alludes to the moment of death, which in effect is instantaneous: the person who is struck—even if only superficially, on the hand or on the ear—falls lifeless immediately, and the corpse shows no sign of trauma, except for a small ring-shaped bruise at the point of contact, along the knall's geometric axis.

A knall can be used only once, then is thrown away. This is a neat, clean town, and knalls are not usually found on the

★ *Max and Moritz (A Story of Seven Boyish Pranks)*, by Wilhelm Busch, is a German children's tale in verse, published in 1865.

sidewalks but only in the garbage cans on street corners and at tram stops. Exploded knalls are darker and more flaccid than unused ones; they are easily recognizable. It's not that they've all been employed for criminal purposes: fortunately, we are still a long way from this. But in certain circles carrying a knall—quite openly, in a breast pocket, or attached to the belt, or behind one ear the way a pork butcher carries a pencil—has become de rigueur. Now, since knalls have an expiration date, like antibiotics or film, many people feel obliged to fire them before they expire, not so much out of prudence as because the firing of a knall has unusual effects, which, though they have been described and studied only in part, are already widely known among consumers. It shatters stone and cement and in general all solid materials—the harder the material the more easily. It pierces wood and paper, sometimes setting them on fire; it melts metals; in water it creates a tiny steaming whirlpool, which, however, disappears immediately. In addition, with a skillfully directed shot one can light a cigarette or even a pipe—a bravura move that, in spite of the disproportionate expense, many young people practice, precisely because of the risk involved. In fact, it has been suggested that this is why the majority of knalls are used for lawful purposes.

The knall is undoubtedly a handy device: it isn't metal, and hence its presence is not detected by common magnetic instruments or X rays; it weighs and costs little; its action is silent, swift, and sure; it's very easy to dispose of. Some psychologists, however, insist that these qualities are not sufficient to explain the knall's proliferation. They maintain that its use would be limited to criminal and terrorist circles if setting it off required a simple movement, such as pressure or friction; however, the knall goes off only if it is maneuvered in a particular way, a precise and rhythmic sequence of twists in one direction and then the other—an operation, in short, that requires skill and dexterity, a little like unlocking the combination of a safe. This operation, it should be noted, is only hinted at but not described in the instructions for use that accompany every box. Therefore, shooting the knall is the object of a secret rite in which initiates indoctrinate neophytes, a rite that has taken on a ceremonial and esoteric character, and is performed in cleverly camouflaged clubs. We might recall here, as an extreme case, the grim discovery that was made in April by the police in F.: in the basement of a restaurant a group of fifteen twelve-year-old boys and a youth of twenty-three were found dead, all clutching in their right hand a discharged knall, and all displaying on the tip of the left ring finger the typical circular bruise.

The police believe that it's better not to draw too much attention to the knall, because doing so would only encourage its spread: this seems to me a questionable opinion, springing, perhaps, from the considerable impotence of the police themselves. At the moment, the only means at their disposal for aid in capturing the biggest knall distributors, whose profits must be monstrous, are informers and anonymous telephone calls.

Being hit by a knall is certainly fatal, but only at close

range; beyond a meter, it's completely harmless, and doesn't even hurt. This feature has had some unusual consequences. Movie-going has decreased significantly, because audience habits have changed: those who go to the movies, alone or in groups, leave at least two seats between them and the other spectators, and, if this isn't possible, often they prefer to turn in their tickets. The same thing happens on the trams, on the subways, and in the stadiums: people, in short, have developed a "crowd reflex," similar to that of many animals, who can't bear the close proximity of others of their kind. Also, the behavior of people on the streets has changed: many prefer to remain at home, or to stay off the sidewalks, thus exposing themselves to other dangers, or obstructing traffic. Many, meeting face to face in hallways or on sidewalks, avoid going around each other, resisting each other like magnetic poles.

The experts have not shown excessive concern about the dangers connected with the widespread use of the knall. They would observe that this device does not spill blood, which is reassuring. In fact, it's indisputable that the great majority of men feel the need, acute or chronic, to kill their neighbor or themselves, but it's not a matter of generic killing: in every instance they have the desire "to shed blood," "to wash away with blood" their own infamy or that of others, "to give their blood" to their country or other institutions. Those who strangle (themselves) or poison (themselves) are much less highly esteemed. In brief, blood, along with fire and wine, is at the center of a grand, glowing-red emotional nexus, vivid in a thousand dreams, poems, and idiomatic expressions: it is sacred and profane, and in its presence man, like the bull and the shark, becomes agitated and fierce. Now, precisely because the knall kills without bloodshed, it's doubtful that it will last. Perhaps that's why, in spite of its obvious advantages, it has not, so far, become a danger to society.

In the Park

It's not hard to imagine who would be waiting for Antonio Casella on the pier: James Collins was waiting for him, in velvet trousers, tanned and relaxed. Antonio wondered whether it would be kinder to ask about the result of his conversation with the publisher or not, but James anticipated him:

"You were quite right—he rejected the manuscript. But he gave me such precise and encouraging suggestions that I immediately began to write again. No, not about you: it's a somewhat fictionalized story about my inventions—their *Entstehungsgeschichte*, their origin, how they occurred to me. Besides, as I see it, it's better for you this way: they told me that you made yourself into a character. Much better—you have a better chance of staying on for a while. My Antonio, in fact, was a little weak."

Antonio listened distractedly: he was too intent on observing the landscape. The boat that brought him had made a long journey up a broad, clear river that ran between thickly forested banks. The current was fast and silent, there was not a breath of wind, the temperature was pleasantly cool, and the forest was as motionless as if made of stone. The water reflected the colors of a sky such as Antonio had never seen: dark blue overhead, emerald green in the east, and violet with wide orange stripes in the west. When the rhythmic rumble of the motor stopped, Antonio became aware of a faint thunder that seemed to saturate the atmosphere. "It's the waterfall," James explained to him. "It's right on the border."

They went along the pier, of rough square blocks, and set off together on a trail that wound its way up around the rampart from which the waterfall cascaded. They were hit by blasts of spray, and the sky was filled with intertwining rainbows. James had politely taken Antonio's suitcase from him; it was very light. Majestic, exotic trees, of many different species, grew on both sides of the path. Flowers hung from the branches, yellow and flesh-colored—some even seemed made of flesh—and trailed in garlands to the ground. There were also fruits, long and rounded; the air held a light, pleasant but slightly musky scent, like that of chestnut blossoms.

At the bar marking the border, no one asked him anything: the two guards saluted him, a hand to their visors, as if they had been expecting him. A little farther on, Antonio entered an office where he was officially registered; a courteous and impersonal functionary checked off his name, handed him a ration card for food, clothes, shoes, and cigarettes, and then said:

"You're an autobiographer, right?"

"Yes. How did you know?"

"We know everything. Look!" He gestured behind him, where a card catalogue occupied an entire wall. "The fact is that at the moment I don't have a single chalet available. The last one we assigned yesterday to Papillon. You'll have to adjust to having a roommate for a few days—another auto-biographer, of course. Here, there's a place at 525, with François Villon. Mr. Collins will show you—it's not very far."

James smiled. "You'll be amused. François is the most unpredictable of our fellow-citizens. He used to live with Julius Caesar, but he got out: he pulled some strings, and was assigned a custom, prefab house on the shores of Lake Polevoy. They didn't get along: they quarreled because of Vercingetorix, then François courted Cleopatra intensely, in Shakespeare's version, and Caesar was jealous."

"What do you mean, in Shakespeare's version?"

"We have five or six Cleopatras: Pushkin's, Shaw's, Gautier's, and so on. They can't stand one another."

"Ah. And so it isn't true that Caesar and Pompey are caulkers?"

"Who ever told you that?" asked James, in amazement.

"Rabelais II, 30. He also says that Hannibal is a chicken seller, Romulus a cobbler, Pope Julius II goes around selling pies, and Livia scrapes the verdigris from the pans."

"That's nonsense. As I told you back in Milan, here people

either do nothing or do the job they were born to. Besides, Rabelais isn't a character, and he's never been here: what he says he must have heard from Pantagruel, or some other fibber in his court."

They had left the waterfall behind and were advancing over a broad, slightly undulating plateau. Suddenly, with incredible speed, the sky darkened; within a few moments a violent whirlwind had arisen, and it began to rain and hail. James explained to Antonio that it was always like this here: the weather was never insignificant. There was always something that made it worthy of description. It was either dazzling with colors and aromas or shaken by raging tempests; sometimes there was scorching heat, at other times rock-splitting cold. Northern lights and earthquakes were frequent, and bolides and meteors fell every night.

They took shelter in a shed, and Antonio realized uneasily that someone was already there: uneasily because the someone didn't have a face. Under his beret only a convex, spongy pink surface was visible, the lower part covered by a badly shaved beard.

"Don't pay any attention to him," said James, who had seen the horror appear on Antonio's face. "There are a lot of them like that here, but they don't last long. They are unsuccessful characters: sometimes they get by for a season, maybe even less. They don't speak, they don't see, and they don't hear, and they disappear in the space of a few months. Those who do last, however, like (we hope) you and me, resemble the weather here—they have something singular about them, and so in general they're interesting and sympathetic, even if they tend to repeat themselves. Here, for example: take a look through that window and tell me if you recognize anyone."

Beside the shed there was a low wooden building with a thatched roof, and on the door hung a sign: on one side had been painted a full moon, and on the other a stormy sea from which emerged the broad back of a whale with its tall spout of vapor. Through the window you could see a smoky, low-ceilinged interior, illuminated by oil lamps: there was a table in the foreground, littered with mugs of beer, both empty and full, and around it four hot, excited figures. From outside one could hear only an indistinct roar.

Antonio, inspired by his ambitions as a reader, considered for a long time but couldn't figure it out. "You're asking too much. If I could at least hear what they're saying . . ."

"Of course I'm asking too much. But it was only to give you a preliminary idea of our environment. The thin balding one with his back to us, who pays and doesn't drink, is Calandrino;★ opposite him, the fat greasy one, with the three days' beard, is the Good Soldier Sweik, who drinks and doesn't pay. The elderly fellow on the left, with the top hat and those tiny eyeglasses, is Pickwick, and the last, with eyes like coals, skin like leather, and his shirt unbuttoned, who doesn't drink and doesn't pay, doesn't sing, doesn't pay attention to the others, and says things that no one is listening to, is the Ancient Mariner."

★ The hero of several stories in Boccaccio's *Decameron*.

As suddenly as it had darkened, the sky cleared, and a fresh, warm wind arose; the wet earth exhaled an iridescent fog that the breeze tore to shreds, and it dried up in a flash. The two resumed their walk. On both sides of the street appeared, in no apparent order, thatched huts and noble marble palaces, villas great and small, shady parks, temple ruins, giant housing projects with laundry hung out to dry, skyscrapers and tin-and-cardboard hovels. James pointed out to Antonio the garden of the Finzi-Contini, the house of Buddenbrooks and that of Usher side by side; Uncle Tom's cabin and the Castle of Verona with the falcon, the deer, and the black horse. A little beyond, the road widened into a small paved square, surrounded by dark, grimy buildings; through the entrances one could see steep, dank stairways, and courtyards full of rubbish, ringed by rusty balconies. There was an odor of boiled cabbage, of lye, and of fog. Antonio immediately recognized a neighborhood of old Milan, or, more precisely, the Carrobio, caught for eternity as it must have been two hundred years ago; he was trying in the uncertain light to decipher the faded signs of the shops when, from the doorway numbered *vottcentvott*, Giovannino Bongeri★ himself jumped out, lean, quick, pale as one who never sees the sun, cheerful, chattering, and as eager for affection as an ill-treated puppy: he wore a tight, ragged suit, somewhat patched, but meticulously clean and pressed. He immediately addressed the two men with the

★ Hero of a poem by Carlo Porta (1775–1821), "Desgressi de Giovannin Bongee" ("The Misadventures of Giovannino Bongeri"), written in the Milanese dialect. (*Vottcentvott* is dialect for "eight hundred and eight.")

ease of an old acquaintance, yet called them "Most Illustri-
ous": he made a long speech in dialect, full of digressions,
which Antonio understood half of and James didn't understand at all; it seemed that he had been wronged, and had
been wounded, but not to the point of losing his dignity as a
citizen and an artisan; he was angry, but not to the point of
losing his head. In his speech, which was witty and long-
winded, one heard, under the bruising grind of daily toil,
poverty, and misfortune, genuine candor, solid human goodness, and ancient hope. Antonio, in a flash of intuition, saw
that in the phantoms of that neighborhood lived something
perfect and eternal, and that angry little Giovannino, the
junkman's helper, repeatedly beaten, mocked, and betrayed—
son of the angry little Milanese Carletto Porta—was a purer,
fuller character than Solomon in all his glory.

While Giovannini spoke, Barberina came to join him, pink
and white as a flower, with lace cap and filigree hat pins, her
eyes a little keener than honesty calls for. Her husband took
her under the arm and off they went toward La Scala: after a
few steps the woman turned and shot the two strangers an
inquisitive glance.

Antonio and James started off again on a dusty path
between bramble hedges: James delayed a moment to greet
Valentino in his new clothes, playing on a stunted lawn with
Pin di Carrugio Lungo.* A little farther on, the path followed

* Valentino is the little boy in the poem "Valentino," by Giovanni Pascoli
(1855–1912), from the collection *Canti di Castel Vecchio*; Pin di Carrugio
Lungo is the hero of Italo Calvino's *The Path to the Spiders' Nest*.

a bend in a big muddy river. A rusty broken-down steamer was anchored near the bank. A group of white men were burying something in a grave dug in the mud, and an insolent-looking black man stuck his head up above the trench and announced, with fierce disdain, "Mistah Kurtz—he dead." The tone of that voice, the setting, the silence, the heat, even the heavy swamp breath of the river were precisely what Antonio had always imagined.

He said to James, "It's clear that one wouldn't get bored here. But what about practical needs? If, for example, one had to have a shoe resoled, or a tooth pulled?"

"We have some modest social services," James answered, "and the medical system is efficient, but with staff from the outside. It isn't that there's a shortage of doctors here, but they don't practice willingly. Often they are of an antiquated school, or they lack the equipment, or, again, they ended up here through some famous mistake—precisely what made them problematic, and therefore characters. Besides, you'll soon see that the sociology of the park is peculiar. I don't think you'll find a baker or an accountant; as far as I know, there's one milkman, a single naval engineer, and a sole spinner of silk. You'll look in vain for a plumber, an electrician, a welder, a mechanic, or a chemist, and I wonder why. Instead, in addition to the doctors I mentioned, you'll find a flood of explorers, lovers, cops and robbers, musicians, painters, and poets, countesses, prostitutes, warriors, knights, foundlings, bullies, and crowned heads. Prostitutes above all, in a percentage absolutely disproportionate to actual need. In short, it's better not to seek here an image of the world you left. I mean, a faithful image: because you'll find one, yes, but multicolored, dyed, and distorted, and so you'll realize how foolish it is to form a concept of the Rome of the Caesars through Virgil, Catullus, and *Quo Vadis*. Here you will not find a sea captain who has not been shipwrecked, a wife who has not been an adulteress, a painter who does not live in poverty for long years and then become famous. Just like the sky, which here is always spectacular. Especially the sunsets: often they last from early afternoon until night, and sometimes darkness falls and then the light returns and the sun sets again, as if it were granting an encore."

James interrupted his lecture to point out to Antonio an edifice they were approaching:

"Sooner or later the Michelin Guide to the Park will come out, and you'll see, this will have three stars." It was a dazzling white villa, or maybe a tiny fortress, immersed in the thick foliage of an old forest: the outer walls had no windows, and were topped with a jagged edge that might be a battlement.

"Seen from the outside it doesn't look like much, but you should see the inside. I've been there for a few small jobs—as I told you, plumbers are scarce, so I do my best—and I could tell you some stories. Do you know, the management has been trying to please the proprietress for six hundred years, without success? Only now, with modern technology . . ."

"Excuse me," Antonio interrupted, a bit annoyed, "but if you told me who the proprietress is, don't you think I would enjoy your discourse more?".

"Oh, I thought I'd told you. It's Beatrice, damn it. The angelic, monstrous Beatrice, who wants everyone at her service, never goes out, speaks to no one, eats only pre-frozen nectar and ambrosia, and, with the protection that she enjoys, there is no hope of getting rid of her, not now or in the foreseeable future. As I was just saying, only now, with the advent of plastics and electronics, have the directors managed to satisfy some of her whims. Look inside: it's a concentrated version of the Fair of Milan, without all the commotion, of course. She walks only on polyurethane foam, a meter thick, like a pole vaulter: barefoot, naturally, and swathed in nylon veils. No daylight: only neon, in pink, purple, and sky-blue; an orgy of false skies made of methacrylate, false fixed stars made of hastelloy, false music of the spheres performed on an electronic organ, false closed-circuit TV visions, false pharmacological ecstasies, and a Prime Mover of Pyrex that cost three million lire a square meter. In short, she is unbearable. But when you're a character from Dante, you're untouchable here. In my opinion, it's a typical Mafioso set up: why should Paolo and Francesca continue to make love undisturbed (and not only in the whirlwind, believe me), while the Poor Lovers[*] have endless difficulties with the park guards? Why is Cacciaguida[†] in the chalet at the top of the hill and Somacal,[‡]

[*] A reference to the novel *Le Cronache di Poveri Amanti* (*Chronicle of Poor Lovers*) by Vasco Pratolini (1913–91).

[†] Dante's great-great-grandfather, who appears in Paradiso XV, XVI, and XVIII.

[‡] A reference to the poem "Il Soldato Somacal Luigi" ("The Soldier Luigi Somacal") by Piero Jahier (1884–1966).

who's been through so much, down in the hut that never gets the sun?"

Because he was so busy talking, James had lost his breath, and also the way. "We'll have to ask someone."

"Do you know everyone here?"

"We almost all know each other. Basically, there aren't so many of us."

He knocked at the door of a wooden hut and went in. Smoke was rising from the chimney, and through the walls a strongly rhythmic martial song could be heard, but he came out again shortly. "They're nice, but they never leave home, and they couldn't give me any directions. They're also a bit timid. Who are they? The little Germans of *All Quiet on the Western Front*: Tjaden, Kat, Leer, and all the others; also Paul Bäumer, naturally. I often go and visit them—what fine boys! They were lucky to come here as young men; otherwise, who knows how many of them would have had to take up arms again twenty years later, and lose either their skin or their soul."

Fortunately, soon afterward they met Babalaci, who knew everything: where François's chalet was, that there was in fact an empty bed, how long it had been empty, why and how, all those with whom François had quarreled recently, and all the women he had received.

In that area the sky was the color of lead; a damp angry wind blew, howling around the corners like a wolf, and in fact when the chalet came into view snow began to fall: dirty snow, gray and sooty, which came down at a slant, got in your eyes, and took your breath away. Antonio couldn't wait to get inside, but James told him it would be better if he waited a little distance away: François was a lunatic type, and James preferred to knock on the door alone; a new face might set him off.

Antonio took cover as well as he could; there was a pile of broken barrels nearby, and he got into a tub and huddled inside to wait for James to return. He saw him knock, wait a good two minutes, knock again: the shutters were closed, but thick smoke was rising from the chimney so there must be someone home.

James knocked a third time, and finally the door was opened. James disappeared inside, and Antonio realized that he was very tired, and began to wonder if it would be possible to have a warm bath: on the banks of the Congo he had sweated a lot, the dust had stuck to his clothes, and now the sweat was cooling on him unpleasantly. But he didn't have long to wait: the door burst open as if someone inside had fired a cannon, and the worthy and dignified James shot out like a meteor, and landed among the barrel staves, not far from Antonio's temporary abode. He got up and quickly brushed himself off:

"No, no, please don't be upset. I happened in at a bad moment—he was with some friends who needed to be handled with care. There was also Marion l'Ydolle, La Grosse Margot, Jehanne di Bretaigne,* and two or three other girls;

* Characters in poems by Villon.

one it seemed to me was the Maid of Orleans. Listen, for the future we'll see, but tonight come and sleep with me: there's not much room, but I'll happily give you the bed, and for me a mattress on the floor is just fine."

ANTONIO SETTLED in to the park with surprising ease. In a few weeks, he had made friends with his neighbors, all cordial people, or at least varied and interesting: Kim with his sword, Iphigenia in Aulis, Ettore Fieramosca, Tommasino Puzzilli, who was engaged to Moll Flanders, Holden Caulfield, Commissioner Ingravallo, Alyosha with the Pious One, Sergeant Grisha with Lilian Aldwinkle, Bel Ami, Alberto da Giussano, who was with the Virgin Camilla, Professor Unrat with the Blue Angel, Leopold Bloom, Mordo Nahum, Justine with Dracula, St. Augustine with the Novice, the two dogs Flush and Buck, Baldus who couldn't get through doors, Benito Cereno, Lesbia living with Hot-Blooded Paolo,* Tristram Shandy who was still only two and a half, Thérèse Raquin and Bluebeard. At the end of the

---

* Ettore Fieramosca is the hero of the eponymous novel of 1833 by Massimo d'Azeglio; Tommasino Puzzilli is the hero of Pasolini's *A Violent Life* (1959); Commissioner Ingravallo is a character in Carlo Emilio Gadda's *That Awful Mess on Via Merulana* (1957); Sergeant Grisha is from Arnold Zweig's *Sergeant Grisha* (1928) and Lilian Aldwinkle is from Huxley's *Those Barren Leaves* (1925); Bel Ami refers to Maupassant's novel; Alberto da Giussano was a legendary Lombard fighter of the twelfth century and the Roman martyr Camilla appears in the Aeneid; Mordo Nahum is a character in Levi's *The Truce*; Baldus is the hero of a sixteenth-century poem; Hot-Blooded Paolo is the eponymous hero of the novel *Paolo il Caldo* (1964) by Vitaliano Brancati.

month Portnoy arrived, crass and complaining: no one could bear him, but in the space of a few days he had settled in Semiramis'★ house, and the rumor went around that things between them were steaming right along.

Antonio moved in with Horace, and was very comfortable there: he had different habits and hours, but he was clean, discreet, and tidy, and he had welcomed him gladly; furthermore, he had a lot of odd stories to tell, and he told them with an enchanting enthusiasm. And, in turn, Horace never seemed to tire of listening to Antonio: he was interested in everything, and up to date even on the most recent events. He was an excellent listener: he seldom interrupted and only with intelligent questions.

Some three years after his arrival, Antonio noticed a surprising fact. When he raised his hands, as a shield against the sun, say, or even against a bright lamp, the light filtered through them as if they were wax. Some time later, he observed that he was waking earlier than usual in the morning, and he realized that this was because his eyelids were more transparent; in fact, in a few days they were so transparent that even with his eyes closed Antonio could distinguish the outlines of objects.

At first he thought nothing of it, but toward the end of May he noticed that his entire skull was becoming diaphanous. It was a bizarre and alarming sensation: as if his field of vision were broadening, not only laterally but also up, down, and

★ Semiramis is the Queen of Assyria who had her husband executed in order to become the sole ruler.

backward. He now perceived light no matter what direction it came from, and soon he was able to distinguish what was happening behind him. When, in mid-June, he realized that he could see the chair he was sitting on, and the grass under his feet, Antonio understood that his time had come: the memory of him was extinct and his testimony complete. He felt sadness, but neither fear nor anguish. He took leave of James and his new friends, and sat under an oak to wait for his flesh and his spirit to dissolve into light and wind.

PART II

LATER
STORIES

The Magic Paint

For many years now I have been engaged in the manufacture of paints and, more precisely, their formulation: from this art I earn my sustenance and support my family. It's an ancient and noble art: the earliest reference appears in Genesis 6:14, where it is related how, in obedience to an exact specification on the part of the Almighty, Noah (probably using a brush) covered the Ark, inside and out, with pitch. But it's also a subtly fraudulent art, which tends to hide the substratum, endowing it with the color and the appearance of what it is not: in this it is related to the arts of makeup and costume, which are equally equivocal and equally ancient (Isaiah 3:16 ff).

The most varied demands are constantly being made on those who practice this profession of ours: paints that do not conduct electricity and paints that do, paints that transmit heat or reflect it, that keep mollusks from adhering to hulls, that absorb sound, or that can be removed from a surface like a peel from a banana. People require paints that keep feet from slipping, as for airport steps, and others as slippery as possible, as for the bottoms of skis. We are therefore a versatile people, with vast experience, who are accustomed to both success and the lack of it, and are difficult to surprise.

Nonetheless, we were surprised by a request that came from our agent in Naples, Signor Amato Di Prima: he was pleased to inform us that an important client in his area had experimented with a paint that provided protection from misfortune, and would profitably replace horn amulets, hunchbacks, four-leaf clovers, and charms in general. It had not been possible to glean other information, except for the price, which was very high; he had, however, managed to obtain a sample, which he had already sent by mail. Given the exceptional interest of the product, he urgently beseeched us to devote the greatest attention to the problem, declared his faith in a quick response, and extended his most sincere greetings.

This business, of the miraculous sample that arrives in the mail, along with an urgent prayer to devote et cetera (that is, without resorting to euphemism, to copy it), is part of our work, and constitutes perhaps its most obscure aspect. We would like to do things our own way: make our own choice, of a refined and elegant problem, take off on the hunt, sight the solution, pursue it, corner it, spear it, strip it of everything inessential, make it in the laboratory, then manufacture it on a small scale, and finally go into full production and get money and glory from it. But that almost never happens. There are many of our kind in this world, and our colleagues and rivals in Italy, in America, in Australia, in Japan are not exactly dozing. We are awash in samples, and we would happily yield to the temptation to throw them away or return them to the sender, were it not for the consideration that our own products suffer the same fate, becoming, in their turn, marvelous, being shrewdly seized and smuggled out by the agents of our competitors, scrutinized, analyzed, and copied: some badly, others well—by the addition, that is, of a particle of originality and genius. Thus begins an endless network of espionage and cross-fertilization, which, illuminated by solitary creative flashes, constitutes the foundation of technological progress. In short, the samples of the competition cannot be thrown out with the dregs: one must see what's there, even if the professional conscience puts up a struggle.

The paint that came from Naples, at first glance, did not display any special property: appearance, odor, drying time were those of a common clear acrylic enamel, and the whole business stank of a hoax. I telephoned Di Prima, who was indignant: he was not the type to send samples around just for fun, and that one in particular had cost him time and trouble—the product was extremely interesting and in his market he was having incredible success. Technical documentation? It didn't exist, there was no need for it, the effectiveness of the product spoke for itself. A fishing boat had been coming back with empty nets for three months—they had painted its hull and ever since it had been netting spectacular catches. A typographer had mixed the paint with printing ink: the ink didn't go as far, but the typographical errors had disappeared. If somehow we were unable to use it, we should tell him immediately; otherwise, we should get busy with it. The price was 7,000 lire a kilo, which seemed to him a good profit margin, and he would undertake to sell at least twenty tons a month.

I talked about it with Chiovatero, who is a serious and capable fellow. At first he turned up his nose, then he thought about it, and proposed starting simply; that is, trying the paint on cultures of *E. coli* bacteria. What did he expect? That the cultures would multiply more than the controls or less? Chiovatero was annoyed, and told me that it was not his habit to put the cart before the horse (implying, by this, that it was *my* habit, which, for goodness' sake, is absolutely not true), that it remained to be seen, that you had to start somewhere, and that "the load adjusts along the way." He obtained the cultures, painted the outside of the test tubes, and we waited. None of us were biologists, but no biologist was needed to interpret the results. After five days, the effect was obvious: the protected cultures had developed in size at three times the rate of the controls, which we had coated with an acrylic ostensibly similar to the one from Naples. We had to conclude that this paint "brought good luck" even to microorganisms: an irritating conclusion, but, as has been authoritatively stated, facts are obstinate. A more thorough analysis was required, but everyone knows what a complex and uncertain enterprise the examination of a paint is: almost like that of a living organism.

All those fantastic modern devices—the infrared spectrum, the gas chromatograph, NMR—are helpful to a point but leave many angles unexplored; and if you aren't lucky enough to have a metal as the key component, all you can do is use your nose, like a dog. But in this case there *was* a metal: an unusual metal, so unusual that no one in the laboratory knew from experience how it reacted. We had to burn almost the entire sample to obtain a quantity sufficient for identification; but finally we did and it was duly confirmed, with all its characteristic reactions. It was tantalum, a very respectable metal, with a name full of meaning, never before seen in paint, and thus surely responsible for the property that we were looking for. As always happens once you've made a finding and confirmed it, the presence of tantalum, and its specific function, began to seem gradually less strange, and, finally, natural, just as no one is surprised anymore by X rays. Molino pointed out that the most acid-resistant reaction vessels are made with tantalum; Palazzoni recalled that tantalum is used to make surgical prostheses that absolutely can't be rejected; and so we concluded that it is an obviously beneficial metal, and that we had been foolish to waste so much time on analyses. With a little common sense we should have been able to think of it right off.

In a few days we got a soap of tantalum, put it in some paint, and tried it on the *E. coli*: it worked, the goal was achieved.

We, in turn, sent a large sample of paint to Di Prima, so that he could distribute it to his customers and give us an opinion. The opinion arrived two months later, and was highly favorable: he, Di Prima, had painted himself from head to foot, and then had spent four hours under a ladder, on a Friday, in the company of thirteen black cats, without coming to any harm. Chiovatero also tried it, albeit reluctantly (not because he was superstitious; rather because he was skeptical), and he had to admit that a certain effect was undeniable: in the two or three days after the treatment, all the traffic lights he came to were green, he never got a busy signal on the telephone, his girlfriend made up with him, and he even won a modest prize in the lottery. Naturally it all came to an end after he took a bath.

As for me, I thought of Michele Fassio. Fassio is an old schoolmate of mine to whom mysterious powers had been attributed since adolescence. He was blamed for endless disasters, from failed exams to a bridge collapse, an avalanche, even a shipwreck: all due, in the stupid opinion of, first, his fellow-students and, later, his colleagues, to the penetrating power of his evil eye. I, of course, didn't believe this nonsense, but I confess that I often tried to avoid running into him. Fassio, poor fellow, ended up believing it himself, in a way; he never married and he led an unhappy life, of privation and solitude. I wrote to him, with all the delicacy I was capable of, that I didn't believe in this type of foolishness, but that he might; that, as a result, I couldn't believe in the remedy I was proposing, but it seemed to me that I owed it to him to mention it just the same, if only to help him recover his self-confidence. Fassio answered that he would come as soon as possible: he was willing to submit to a trial. Before proceeding with the treatment, and at the urging of Chiovatero, we tried to understand in some degree Fassio's powers. We managed to ascertain that in fact his gaze (and only his gaze) possessed a specific effect, noticeable under certain conditions even in the case of inanimate objects. We asked him to stare for several minutes at a particular point on a steel plate, which we then placed in the salt-spray chamber; after a few hours we noted that the point Fassio had stared at was clearly more corroded than the rest of the surface. A polyethylene thread, stretched tight, consistently broke at the point where Fassio's gaze hit it. To our satisfaction, both results disappeared when we coated the plate and the thread with our paint, or when we interposed between subject and object a glass screen previously coated with it. We were further able to ascertain that only Fassio's right eye was active: the left, like both of my eyes, and like Chiovatero's, exercised no measurable action. With the means at our disposal, we were unable to carry out a spectral analysis of the Fassio effect except in a crude way; it is probable, however, that the radiation under examination has a maximum in the blue, with a wavelength of around 425 Nm. Our exhaustive paper on the subject will be out in a few months. Now, it is known that many of those who wish to cast the evil eye wear blue-tinted lenses, and not dark ones, and this can't be a coincidence but must, rather, be the fruit of long experience absorbed perhaps unconsciously and then handed down from generation to generation, as in the case of certain folk remedies.

Considering the tragic conclusion of our tests, I have to explain that the idea of painting Fassio's eyeglasses (they were ordinary reading glasses) was neither mine nor Chiovatero's but came from Fassio himself, who insisted that the experiment be made right away, without even an hour's delay: he was very impatient to be released from his grim power. We painted these glasses. After thirty minutes the paint was dry: Fassio put them on and immediately fell lifeless at our feet. The doctor, who arrived soon afterward, tried in vain to revive him, and spoke vaguely of embolism, heart attack, and thrombosis: he couldn't have known that the lens over Fassio's right eye, concave on the inside, must have instantaneously reflected that thing which he could no longer transmit, and must have concentrated it, as if with a burning glass, on a point situated in some unspecified but important corner of the right cerebral hemisphere of the unhappy and blameless victim of our experiments.

Gladiators

Nicola would happily have stayed home, and even in bed until ten, but Stefania wouldn't hear of it. At eight, she was already on the phone: she reminded him that he had been making excuses for far too long. Sometimes it was the rain, sometimes it was the contestants, who were mediocre, sometimes he had to go to a meeting, and sometimes there were his silly humanitarian excuses. Noticing in his voice a shadow of reluctance, or, perhaps, only of a bad mood, she ended by telling him outright that promises are made to be kept. She was a girl with many virtues, but when she got an idea in her head there was no way around it. Nicola didn't recall having made her an actual promise. He had said, vaguely, that yes, someday they would go to the stadium—all his colleagues went, and also (alas!) all her colleagues. Every Friday they filled in betting forms for the gladiator contest, and he had agreed with her that one shouldn't set oneself apart, give oneself the airs of an intellectual; and then it was an experience, a curiosity that, once in your life, you needed to satisfy, otherwise you don't know the world you're living in. Yet now that it had come to the point, he realized that he had made all those speeches with some mental reservation—he had no desire to actually see the gladiators and never would. On the other hand, how to say no to Stefania? He would pay dearly, he knew: with insults, sulks, rebuffs. Maybe even worse—there was that fair-haired cousin of his . . .

He shaved, washed, dressed, went out. The streets were deserted, but there was already a line at the store on Via San Secondo. He hated lines, but he got on the end of it just the same. The advertisement was hanging on the wall, in the usual garish colors. There were six entrants; the names of the gladiators meant nothing to him, except that of Turi Lorusso. Not that he knew much about Lorusso's technique; he knew that he was good, that he was paid an enormous sum, that he slept with a countess, and perhaps also with the relevant count, that he gave a lot to charity and paid no taxes. While Nicola waited his turn, he listened in on the conversations of his neighbors.

"If you ask me, after thirty years they shouldn't allow it anymore . . ."

"Of course, the acceleration, the eye aren't what they used to be, but, on the other hand, he has experience of the arena that . . ."

"But did you see him, in '91, against that madman who drove the Mercedes? When he threw the hammer from twenty meters and hit him straight on? And remember the time they ejected him for . . .?"

He bought two tickets for the grandstand: it wasn't the moment to worry about cost. He went home and telephoned Stefania: he would pick her up at two.

By three the stadium was full. The first entry was scheduled for three, but still at three-thirty nothing had happened. Near them sat a white-haired old man with a deep tan. Nicola asked him if the delay was normal.

"They always make you wait. It's incredible—they act like prima donnas. In my time it was different. Instead of foam-rubber bumpers there were beaks—no nonsense. It was hard to escape without injury. Only the top players managed it, the ones who were born with combat in their blood. You're young, you don't remember the champions who came out of Pinerolo's stable, and, even better, Alpignano's. Now, can you believe it? They're all from reformatories or from the New Prisons, or even from the prison for the criminally insane: if they accept, their sentence is commuted. It's laughable now, they have insurance, disability, paid holidays, and after fifty fights they even get a pension. Oh, yes, there are some who retire at forty."

A murmur rose from the bleachers, and the first man entered. He was very young: he appeared confident but you could see he was afraid. Immediately afterward a flame-red Fiat 127 came into the ring; the three ritual honks of the horn sounded, and Nicola felt the nervous grip of Stefania's hand on his biceps; the car aimed straight at the boy, who waited in a slight crouch, tense, legs wide, gripping the hammer convulsively in his fist. Suddenly the auto accelerated, its tractor wheels spewing two jets of sand in its wake. The boy dodged and struck a blow, but too late: the hammer just grazed the side, denting it slightly. The driver must not have had much imagination; there were several more such charges, extremely monotonous, then the gong sounded and the round concluded with no decision.

The second gladiator (Nicola glanced at the program) was called Blitz, and he was stocky and smooth-skinned. There were several skirmishes with the Alfasud compact car that he had drawn as an adversary; the man was skillful enough and managed to keep wide of it for two or three minutes, then the car hit him, in first gear but hard, and he was thrown a dozen meters. His head was bleeding; the doctor came, declared him incapacitated, and the stretcher-bearers carried him off amid the catcalls of the spectators. Nicola's neighbor was outraged. He said that Blitz, whose real name, by the way, was Craveri, was an impostor, that he got himself injured on purpose, that he should change careers—in fact, the Federation should change careers for him: take away his license and put him back in the ranks of the unemployed.

In the case of the third, who was also up against an economy car, a Renault 4, he pointed out that these cars were more dangerous than the big heavy cars. "If it was up to me, I would make them all Mini Morrises. They have acceleration, and they handle well. With those monsters of 1600 and up, nothing ever happens. They're fine for newcomers—just smoke in their eyes." At the third charge, the gladiator waited for the auto without moving: at the last instant he threw himself flat on the ground and the car drove over him without touching him. The spectators shouted with enthusiasm; many of the women threw flowers and purses into the arena, and even a shoe, but Nicola learned that that move, though it looked impressive, wasn't really dangerous. It was called "the Rudolf," because a gladiator named Rudolf had invented it: he had later become famous, had had a political career, and was now a big shot on the Olympic Committee.

Next, there was the usual comic interlude: a duel between two forklifts. They were the same model and color but one had a red stripe painted on it and the other a green stripe. Because they were so heavy, they were difficult to maneuver, sinking into the sand almost up to their hubs. In vain they tried to push each other back, with their forks entwined like battling stags; then the green stripe disentangled itself, backed up rapidly, and, making a tight turn, butted the side of red with its rear. Red yielded but then quickly went into reverse and managed to lodge its fork under the belly of green. The fork rose, and green swayed and then fell on one side, indecently exposing its differential and muffler. The audience laughed and applauded.

The fourth gladiator had to go against a banged-up Peugeot. The crowd immediately began to shout "Rigged!" The driver even had the audacity to switch on his turn signal before swerving.

The fifth entry was a real spectacle. The gladiator was gutsy and was obviously aiming not just at the windshield but at the head of the driver, and he missed by a hair. He dodged three charges, with precision and lazy grace, not even raising the hammer; at the fourth, he bounced up in front of the car like a spring, came down on the hood, and with two brutal hammer blows shattered the windshield. Nicola heard a brief, strangled cry that stood out from the roar of the crowd: it was Stefania, who was pressed tight against him. The driver seemed to be blinded: instead of braking, he accelerated and hit the wooden barrier sideways; the car rebounded and came to rest on its side, trapping one of the gladiator's feet in the sand. He was mad with rage, and continued, through the empty frame of the windshield, to pound the head of the driver, who was trying to get out of the car by the door facing up. Finally he emerged, his face bleeding; he tore the hammer away from the gladiator, and began wringing his neck. The crowd yelled a word that Nicola couldn't understand, but his neighbor calmly explained to him that they were asking the director of the competition to spare his life, which in fact was what happened. A tow truck from the automobile club entered the arena, and in a flash the car was turned rightside up and towed away. The driver and the gladiator shook hands amid the applause, and then walked toward the locker rooms waving, but after a few steps the gladiator staggered and fell. It wasn't clear if he was dead or had only fainted. They loaded him, too, onto the tow truck.

As the great Lorusso entered the arena, Nicola realized that Stefania had turned very pale. He felt a vague rancor toward her, and he would have liked to stay longer, if only to make her pay—he couldn't care less about Lorusso. On principle he would have preferred Stefania to ask him if they could leave, but he knew her, and knew that she would never stoop to that, so he told her that he had had enough, and they left. Stefania didn't feel well, she felt like throwing up, but when he questioned her she said curtly that it was the sausage she had eaten at dinner. She refused to have a glass of bitters at the bar, refused to spend the evening with him, rebuffed every topic of conversation that he suggested: she really must be ill. Nicola took her home, and realized that he, too, had little appetite, and didn't even feel like playing the usual game of pool with Renato. He drank two cognacs and went to bed.

The Fugitive

To compose a poem that is worth reading and remembering is a gift of destiny: it happens to only a few people, without regard for rules or intentions, and to them it happens only a few times in their lives. Perhaps this is a good thing; if the phenomenon were more frequent, we would be drowning in poetic messages, our own and those of others, to the detriment of us all. To Pasquale, too, it had happened only a few times, and the awareness of having a poem in his mind, ready to be caught in flight and fixed on a page like a butterfly, had always been accompanied by a curious sensation, by an aura like that which precedes epileptic fits: each time, he had heard a faint whistle in his ears, and a ticklish shiver ran through him from head to foot.

In a few moments the whistle and the shiver disappeared, and he found himself clear-headed, with the core of the poem lucid and distinct; he had only to write it down, and, lo and behold, the other lines hastened to crowd around it, obedient and strong. In a quarter of an hour the work was done: but this flash, this instantaneous process in which conception and birth succeeded one another almost like lightning and thunder, had been granted to Pasquale only five or six times in his life. Luckily, he wasn't a poet by profession: he had a dull, boring office job.

He felt the symptoms described above after two years of silence, as he was sitting at his desk, examining an insurance policy. In fact, he felt them with an unusual intensity: the whistle was penetrating and the shiver was a nearly convulsive tremor, which disappeared immediately, leaving him with a sensation of vertigo. The key verse was there before him, as if written on the wall, or, rather, inside his skull. His colleagues at the neighboring desks didn't notice anything. Pasquale concentrated fiercely on the sheet of paper in front of him: from the core the poem radiated out through all his senses like a growing organism, and soon it was before him; it seemed to be throbbing, just like a living thing.

It was the most beautiful poem that Pasquale had ever written. There it was, right before his eyes, without a correction, the handwriting tall, elegant, and smooth: it was almost as if the sheet of copy paper on which it was written had difficulty bearing its weight, like a column too slender beneath the burden of a giant statue. It was six o'clock: Pasquale locked the poem in his drawer and went home. It seemed to him that he deserved a reward, and on the way he bought himself an ice cream.

The next morning he rushed to the office. He was impatient to reread the poem, because he was well aware how hard it is to judge a newly written work: the value and the meaning, or the lack of value and meaning, become clear only the morning after. He opened the drawer and didn't see the page: and yet he was sure that he had left it on top of all the other papers. He dug around among them, frantically at first, then methodically, but he had to admit that the poem had disappeared. He searched the other drawers, and then he realized that the poem was right there in front of him, on the in-box tray. What tricks distraction plays! But how could he not be distracted, in the face of the ultimate work of his life?

PASQUALE WAS certain that his future biographers would remember him for nothing else: only for that "Annunciation." He reread it and was enthusiastic, almost in love. He was about to take it to the photocopying machine when the boss called him in; he kept him for an hour and a half, and when Pasquale returned to his desk the copier was broken. By four o'clock the electrician had repaired it, but the photocopying paper was all used up. For that day there was nothing to be done: recalling the incident of the previous evening, Pasquale placed the sheet of paper in the drawer with great care. He closed it, then changed his mind and opened it, and finally he closed it again and left. The next day the piece of paper wasn't there.

This business was becoming annoying. Pasquale turned all

his drawers upside down, bringing to light papers that had been forgotten for decades: as he searched, he tried to retrieve in memory if not the whole composition at least that first line, that nucleus which had enlightened him, but he couldn't: in fact, he had the precise sensation that he never would. He was different, different from that moment on: he was no longer the same Pasquale, and he never would be again, just as a dead man does not return to life, and you never put your foot in the same river twice. There was a nauseating metallic taste in his mouth: the taste of frustration, of nevermore. Disconsolate, he sat down in his office chair, and saw the page stuck to the wall, to his left, a little distance from his head. It was obvious: some colleague had intended to play a tasteless trick; perhaps someone had been spying on him and was on to his secret.

He seized the sheet of paper by one edge and detached it from the wall, encountering almost no resistance: the author of the trick must have used a poor-quality paste, or used very little. He noticed that the other side of the paper was slightly grainy. He put it under his desk pad, and for the entire morning made excuses not to leave his desk, but when the noon whistle sounded, and everyone got up to go to lunch, Pasquale saw that the sheet of paper was sticking out from under the desk pad by a good inch. He took it out, folded it in fourths, and put it in his wallet: after all, there was no reason not to take it home. He would copy it by hand, or take it to the copy shop; that would solve the problem.

He reread the poem in the evening as he was going home on the subway. Contrary to what he usually felt, it seemed perfect: not a line or a syllable had to be changed. Still, before showing it to Gloria he would think about it. Everyone knows how a judgment can change even in a short time: Monday's masterpiece becomes insipid on Thursday, or even vice versa. He locked the sheet of paper in his private drawer, in the bedroom; but the following morning, when he opened his eyes, he saw it above him, stuck to the ceiling. Two-thirds of it was adhering to the plaster; the other third was hanging down.

Pasquale got the ladder and cautiously removed the piece of paper; again, when he felt it, the surface was rough, especially on the back. He touched it with his lips: there was no doubt, sticking out from the page were some tiny bumps, which seemed to be in rows. He took a magnifying glass and saw that it was so. Tiny hairs were sticking out from the page, corresponding to attributes of the letters on the other side. In particular, the extremities stuck out, the legs of the "d"s and the "p"s, and, above all, the little legs of the "n"s and of the "m"s; for example, behind the title, "Annunciation," the eight legs of the four "n"s could be clearly seen. They stuck out like the whiskers of a badly shaved beard, and it seemed to Pasquale that they even vibrated slightly.

It was time to go to the office, and Pasquale was perplexed. He didn't know where to put the poem. He realized that, for some reason, perhaps precisely because of its uniqueness, because of the life that openly animated it, the poem was trying to escape, to get away from him. He decided to observe it from close up: never mind the office—for once he would be late. Under the magnifying glass he could see that some of the attributes of the letters were surrounded by a thin, clear inlay, in the form of a narrow, elongated U, and were folded back, toward the other side of the paper, in such a way that, if you placed the piece of paper on the surface of the desk, it remained elevated a millimeter or two: he bent down to look, and he could distinctly see the light between the page and the desktop.

And he saw something more: as he watched, the sheet of paper moved in the direction of the title, away from him. It advanced a few millimeters a second, with a slow but uniform and assured motion. He turned it around, so that the title faced away from him; after a few seconds the page took up its march, this time in reverse, that is, toward the opposite edge of the desk.

By now it was getting late; Pasquale had an important appointment at nine-thirty, and he could delay no longer. He went to the storage closet, found a strip of plywood, got the paste, and pasted the wood on top of the piece of paper: "Annunciation" was his work, in the end—his thing, his property. It remained to be seen who was stronger. He went to the office in a rage, and was unable to calm down even in the course of the delicate negotiations that he was in charge of, so that he conducted them in a rude and clumsy manner, and ended up with a deal that was decidedly mediocre, which, naturally, only increased his rage and ill humor. He felt like a race horse yoked to a mill wheel: after two days of walking in a circle are you still a race horse? Do you still have the desire to run, to be first at the finish line? No, you have a desire for silence, rest, and the stable. Luckily at home, at the stable, the poem awaited him. It would no longer escape: how could it?

It had not in fact escaped. He found the remains of it stuck to the piece of wood: twenty little fragments, each no bigger than a postage stamp, for a total area no more than a fifth of the original sheet of paper. The rest of "Annunciation" had departed, in the form of scraps, tiny crumpled, frayed shreds, which were scattered in all the corners of the house: he found only three or four, and though he smoothed them out carefully, they were illegible.

Pasquale spent the following Sunday in less and less reliable efforts to reconstruct the poem. From that time on, there were neither whistles nor shivers; he tried many times, during the rest of his life, to call to memory the lost text; in fact, at increasingly rare intervals, he wrote other versions of it, but they were increasingly thin, bloodless, and weak.

One Night

It was very cold and still. The sun had set a few minutes earlier, sinking obliquely behind a horizon that, owing to the clarity of the air, appeared close, and leaving a luminous yellow-green trail that extended almost to the zenith. Meanwhile in the east the sky was opaque, purplish, obscured by large gray cumuli that seemed to weigh on the frozen land like deflated balloons. The air was dry and smelled like ice.

There was no human trace on the whole plateau except for the train tracks that stretched straight as far as the eye could see and appeared to converge at the point where the sun had just vanished; in the opposite direction they disappeared in the farthest edge of the woods. The land was slightly rolling and covered with small oaks and beeches that the prevailing wind had tilted to the south, bending some of the treetops all the way to the ground. But that day was completely calm. Calcareous rocks whittled by rain and encrusted with fossilized shells appeared on the surface of the ground: rough and white, they looked like the bones of buried animals. From the cracks protruded sticks carbonized by a recent fire. There was no grass, just yellow and red stains of lichen stuck to the rock.

The roar could be heard before the train was visible: in the silence of the plateau, the sound was transmitted through the rock and the ice like underground thunder. The train was fast, and soon one could discern that it was made up of only three boxcars in addition to the engine. When it got closer, the high-pitched drone of the racing diesels could be heard, along with the whistle of air lacerated by its forward motion. The train overtook the observation point in a flash, and both drone and whistle decreased by a tone; it hurtled on between birch trees and the occasional beech on the edge of the woods. Here the tracks were covered by a thick layer of dry, fragile brown leaves. The wave of rushing air collided with the leaves before the train even touched them, lifting them in a scattered cloud—higher than the highest trees, stirred by the gusts of wind like a swarm of bees—that accompanied the train on its course and made it visible from afar. The leaves were light but their mass was large: in spite of its momentum, the train was obliged to slow down.

A shapeless pile of leaves formed in front of the locomotive, which it split in two like a prow: some of the leaves ended up crushed between the tracks and the wheels, increasing the work of the engine and forcing it to slow down even more. At the same time, the friction between the train and the leaves—both the leaves in the piles and the ones that circled about—electrified the air, the train, and the leaves themselves. Large purple sparks streaked from the train to the ground, creating a tangle of luminous fragments against the dark backdrop of the woods. The air was heavy with ozone and the acrid odor of burned paper.

The mass of leaves in front of the locomotive grew thicker and the wheels' grip on the tracks grew weaker until the train stopped, though the engines continued to churn at their maximum strength. The locomotive's wheels, spinning in vain, grew red hot, and even the section of track beneath each wheel became almost incandescent; waves of fire, originating from these incandescent points, rippled over the leaves on the ground, but were spent after a few meters. There was a click, the engines were turned off, and everything was silent again. The face of the engineer appeared at the window of the locomotive, wide and pale: he stared into space, motionless. All the leaves had fallen to the ground. Nothing happened for a long time, but the light crackling of the leaves in front of the locomotive could be heard as they settled back into their position of repose: the pile slowly increased in volume, like rising dough.

Fascinated by the train, some crows had come to rest, and they pecked spitefully at the rocks and the leaves, croaking softly. Just before nightfall they became silent, then all together they took flight; something must have scared them. In fact, from among the trees came a rhythmic rustling, subdued but

widespread: from the woods emerged a group of cautious little people. They were men and women of short stature, slim,
in dark clothes; on their feet they wore coarse felt boots. They
approached the train hesitantly, consulting each other in whis-
pers. They didn't seem to have a leader: nevertheless, determination prevailed over doubt. They gathered around the cars,
and soon the creaking of their weight was followed by a
metallic rustling like that of an anthill that has been disturbed.
The little men and women busied themselves around the
train; they must have had various implements hidden under
their padded jackets, because the indistinct murmur was punc-
tuated by dry crashes and the screech of saws.

Toward sunrise, the steel plates and wood that the cars
were made of had been removed piece by piece and stacked
up beside the tracks, but some of the people, not contented,
attacked the stacks furiously in small groups, with hacksaws,
shears, and hammers: they tore apart, broke up, and destroyed,
as if all order and all structure conflicted with some ideal they
shared. A pile of bits of wood had been set ablaze and the
demolishers took turns standing near it to warm their hands.
Meanwhile, others were occupied with the beams and gird-
ers of the framework; a single individual would not have seen
the end of it in a year, but they were many and they were resolute, and their numbers grew by the hour. Intent and silent
they labored, and the work progressed rapidly: when someone proved unable to destroy a piece, another, more capable
or stronger, would push him aside and take his place. Often
two would quarrel over a piece, tugging on it from opposite

ends. The frames demolished, they busied themselves with the trucks, the shafts, and the wheel disks; it was astonishing how, with such primitive instruments, they managed to get on with their work: they would not abandon a part until it was bent, split, sawed into two unequal parts, splintered, or otherwise rendered unusable.

Demolishing the engine appeared to be more difficult. They worked on it for several hours, taking turns in no apparent order. Many, perhaps to rest, had crammed into the engineer's cab, where a little of the heat from the engines still lingered, but others pulled them out to continue with the work. Soon they formed a chain, starting inside the cab and beside the piles of already removed fragments, and ending in the woods. The unrecognizable segments of the body, of the framework, of the engines, of the electrical system were passed from hand to hand in the uncertain light of dawn; thus, too, the inert body of the engineer. Once the engine, with all its delicate mechanisms, had been dismantled and destroyed, the little people attacked the rails and demolished about a hundred meters in each direction, while others, with great effort, extracted the ties from the frozen ground and split them with axes.

When the sun rose, nothing remained of the train, but the crowd did not disperse; the most vigorous, with those same axes, attacked the bases of the nearest birch trees, felled them, and stripped them of their branches; others, in pairs or in groups, flung themselves against one another with deliberate blows. Some were seen blindly striking themselves.

Fra Diavolo on the Po

~

Before the current confusion of reforms, obtaining a high-school diploma was an undertaking that made one tremble—it was a decathlon. The candidate was required to complete four written exams and an oral exam in every subject covered in three years of high school: in practice, a summary of everything that is known to mankind. Thus, by the day of the first exam, one would be completely exhausted, in a state both frantic and fatalistic, since it was clear to everyone that luck played a major role in the final results.

In July of 1936, precisely two days before my first exam, the written exam in Italian, I received a menacing red postcard from the Ministry of War: the following day I was to report to the seaplane station (the one on the Po River, from which the seaplane leaves for Venice: how many Turinese remember it?) for an urgent message. I went there full of foreboding and found myself in the company of another teen-ager, who (I never discovered why) was also called Levi, before a giant in a Fascist uniform who assailed us with an avalanche of insults, accusations, and threats.

He was red in the face, in a fit of rage; he accused us of nothing less than attempted desertion. We were both cowards: according to him, we hadn't responded to a previous call, clearly intending to avoid military service in the Royal Navy. Yes, because our two names, of all names, had been drawn in the Turin lottery for the Navy draft. No one could save us from twenty-four months of service.

I didn't even know how to swim at the time, and though I had read Stevenson and Defoe, the prospect of becoming a sailor struck me as absurd and frightening. I went home terrified; the next day, I turned in an Italian exam that was insubstantial and incoherent, so much so that, in all fairness, I got a D, was not allowed to take the oral exam, and was told to return in October. It was the first bad grade in my impeccable academic career, and it felt pretty much like a death sentence. I passed the other exams thanks only to an exhausting effort.

WE HELD a family council; my father, poor man, already gravely ill, set about making the rounds of the relevant authorities, from the military recruiting office to the *podestà*,⋆ from

⋆ Chief magistrate.

the Superintendent of Education to the Fascist Federation. What came of it was a paradoxical solution, a preemptive strike: I would avoid the Navy draft by enlisting as soon as possible in the pre-military course at the Milizia Volontaria per la Sicurezza Nazionale,* in other words the Fascist MVSN.

Thus, the following fall, once I had passed my Italian exam, I enrolled in the university and found myself in the position of university soldier. At the time I was neither Fascist nor anti-Fascist. Wearing a uniform gave me no sense of pride; rather, I found it somehow annoying (especially the boots). But I have to admit that I didn't dislike marching in step, in close order, especially to band music. It was a dance, and it gave me the sensation of belonging to a human alliance, of merging with a unified group. I later learned that Einstein declared he could not understand the type of man who took pleasure in marching in step. Well, at the time I was that type, even if seven years later some other marching in step made me change my mind radically.

So there I was, a soldier, all decked out in Alpine hat, eagle, fasces, gray-green jacket and pants, and black shirt. The routine of pre-military education should have enabled me to predict much of what was to come after Italy entered the war, in 1940: suffice it to say that throughout the entire course I neither fired a single shot nor saw even from a distance what the cartridge clips of the extremely heavy Model 91 rifle looked like.

* Volunteer Militia for National Security.

The muster was on Saturday afternoons in the courtyard of the university on Via Po, where, in one of the corridors, the armory of the University Militia was situated. We had to show up in uniform, and each of us was given a rifle; the bayonet—with its two lateral grooves "so that the blood can drain away"—was fixed to the muzzle, and the loop of the bayonet sheath was threaded through the belt, along with cartridge pouches meant to hold ammunition but naturally empty. Once our belts were on we would fill the cartridge pouches with bread and salami for snack time; the smokers used them for cigarettes. Pre-military training consisted solely of the tedious close-order drills and long walks in the hills that would have been pleasant if it hadn't been for the loathsome boots that chafed our ankles and feet raw.

If I am not mistaken, I was the only true university student in my squad. The others were studying geometry or accounting, and had all enrolled in the University Militia for the various worldly advantages that could be gained from it—not one had joined out of Fascist beliefs. Because they were the same height as me, four shrewd, friendly boys—all a little frisky—were always near me in the squad, and with the aid of their rifles they kept themselves entertained by playing the part of Fra Diavolo.* They called each other Canù Vacché

---

* Fra Diavolo (lit. Brother Devil; 1771–1806) was the popular name given to Michele Pezza, a famous Italian outlaw who resisted the French occupation of Naples and is remembered in folk legends and in the novels of Alexandre Dumas as a guerrilla leader. Popular superstition invested him with the character of both monk and demon.

(wizened cowboy), Cravé (Cravero) Bastard,★ Comi Schifús, and Simoncelli Struns:† as in Homeric texts, these were fixed attributes and were an integral part of their names—like honorary titles.

COMI SCHIFÚS in fact was an old acquaintance. He had been a classmate of mine in elementary school, and already then was trying his very best to be gross: he was the only one in our entire class who could lick the soles of his shoes—without taking them off, of course. It pleases me to mention the names of these faraway comrades in arms, in the event that any of them should recognize himself here. One had composed amiably obscene verses in which the surreal names of the parts of the above-mentioned rifle recurred: "dog collar sling," "butt plate," "nose cap," and others I can't recall because, as a matter of fact, we had never taken a rifle apart. The rifle was intended less as a weapon than as a dead weight, useful only for hampering movements.

As a result of the racial laws, my military career didn't last long: in September 1938, I was asked to turn in my uniform, and I did so without regrets. But when, in 1945, I returned from captivity in Germany, I discovered that the specter of military service in the Navy had not vanished: I appeared to still be registered for the naval draft. I was called to the

★ In English in the text.
† *Schifús* is a distorted version of *schifo*, which means disgusting; *Struns* is a distortion of *stronzo*, which literally means turd and is used vulgarly to indicate someone who is mean.

recruiting office to re-state my position, stripped naked, and subjected to the statutory medical exam with the recruits of '27. I was in pretty bad shape, but the doctor wanted to declare me fit for service. A negotiation ensued: strange as it may seem, I did not possess any documents to attest to my year in Auschwitz, except for the number tattooed on my arm. After long explanations and pleading, the doctor agreed first to classify me as temporarily unfit for service, and then to let me out definitively. Thus ended my brief military career.

The Sorcerers

⁓

Wilkins and Goldbaum had been away from their base camp for two days: they had been trying, in vain, to record the dialect of the Siriono* of the east village, on the other side of the river, ten kilometers from the camp and from West Siriono. They saw the smoke and immediately started back: it was a dense black smoke, and it rose slowly into the evening sky, in the very direction where, with the help of the natives, they had built their wood-and-straw huts. They reached the riverbank in less than an hour, forded the muddy stream, and saw the disaster. The camp was no longer there: only smoking embers and scraps of metal, ashes and unidentifiable charred remains.

The village of West Siriono, five hundred meters away, was

* The Siriono are an Indian people who live in the tropical forests of eastern Bolivia.

on a bend in the river; the Siriono were waiting for them, in great excitement: they had tried to put out the fire, drawing water from the river using their crude pots and some buckets, a gift of the two Englishmen, but hadn't managed to salvage anything. Sabotage was unlikely: their relations with the Siriono were good, and, besides, the Siriono weren't that familiar with fire. Probably the generator had backfired—they had left it on during their absence to keep the refrigerator going—or perhaps had had a short circuit. Anyway, the situation was serious: the radio no longer functioned, and the nearest town was a twenty-day walk through the forest.

Up to that point the two ethnographers' contacts with the Siriono had been limited. Only through hard work, and by corrupting him with two cans of corned beef, had they managed to overcome the distrust of Achtiti, who was the most intelligent and curious man in the village; he had consented to answer their questions, speaking into the microphone of the tape recorder. But it had been, rather than a necessity or a job, an academic game: Achtiti, too, had taken it that way, and had obviously found it entertaining to teach the two the names of the colors, of the trees that surrounded the camp, of his friends, and of his women. Achtiti had learned a few words of English, and they a hundred-odd words with a harsh, indistinct sound, and when they tried to reproduce them, Achtiti beat his stomach with both hands in delight.

It was no longer a game. They did not feel capable of following a Siriono guide on a twenty-day march through a forest saturated with putrid water. They would have to explain to Achtiti that he must send a messenger to Candelaria with a letter from them, in which they asked for a motorboat to come up the river to get them, and bring the messenger back to the tribe. It would not be easy to explain to Achtiti even what a letter was. In the meantime, there was nothing to do but ask the Siriono for their hospitality for three or four weeks.

As for hospitality, there were no problems: Achtiti immediately understood the situation, and offered the men a straw pallet, and two of the peculiar Siriono blankets, painstakingly woven from palm fibers and magpie feathers. They put off the explanations till the next day and slept deeply.

The following day, Wilkins prepared the letter for Suarez in Candelaria. He had the idea of drafting it in two versions, one written in Spanish for Suarez and one ideographic, so that both Achtiti and the messenger could get an idea of the purpose of the mission and put aside their evident suspicion. The second version showed the messenger himself walking southwest, along the river; twenty suns were intended to represent the length of the journey. Then came the city: tall huts, and among them many men and women in trousers and skirts and with hats on their heads. Finally, there was a bigger man, pushing the motorboat into the river, with three men on board and sacks of provisions, and the boat going back up the river; in this last image, the messenger was on board, stretched out and eating from a bowl.

Uiuna, the messenger chosen by Achtiti, examined the drawings carefully, asking for explanations with gestures. Was it in the direction that he was pointing to on the horizon? And the distance? Finally he loaded a knapsack of dried meat on his back, took his bow and arrows, and set off barefoot, rapid and silent, with the undulating gait of the Siriono. Achtiti made solemn gestures with his head, as if to say that they could have confidence in Uiuna: Goldbaum and Wilkins looked at one another in bewilderment. It was the first time that a Siriono had traveled so far from the village and gone to a city, in so far as Candelaria, with its five thousand inhabitants, could be considered a city.

Achtiti had food brought to them: shrimp from the river, raw, four each, two japara nuts, and a big fruit with watery, tasteless juice.

Goldbaum said, "Maybe they'll be hospitable, and take care of us even if we don't work. In that case, which would be the most fortunate, they will give us the same ration as theirs, in quality and quantity, and it won't be easy. Or they may ask us to work with them, and we don't know how to hunt or plow. We have almost nothing left to give them. If Uiuna returns without the boat, or doesn't return at all, things will go badly. They'll throw us out, and then we'll die in the swamp; or they'll kill us themselves, as they do with their old people."

"Without warning?"

"I don't think so, and they won't be violent. They'll ask us to follow their custom."

Wilkins was silent for a few minutes, and then he said, "We have two days' worth of provisions, two watches, two ballpoint pens, a lot of useless money, and the tape recorder. Everything in the camp has been destroyed, but we might be able to retemper the knife blades. Ah, yes, we also have two boxes of matches—maybe that's the item that will interest them most. We ought to pay our keep, right?"

The negotiations with Achtiti were laborious. He paid scant attention to the watches, was interested in neither the pens nor the money, and was frightened when he heard his voice come out of the tape recorder. He was fascinated by the matches: after a few failed attempts he was able to light one, but he wasn't convinced that it was a real flame until he held a finger over it and got burned. He lighted another, and declared with evident satisfaction that if he brought it close to the straw it would catch fire. Then he stretched out one hand with a questioning air: could he take all the matches? Goldbaum quickly retrieved them: he showed Achtiti that the box was already partly used up and that the other, though full, was small. He made a gesture that indicated the two of them. He showed Achtiti a match, and then the sun, and the sun's path through the sky: he would give him a match for every day of sustenance. For a long time Achtiti remained in doubt, squatting on his heels, humming in a nasal singsong; then he went into a hut, and came out holding an earthenware bowl and a bow. He placed the bowl on the ground; he picked up some claylike earth, mixed it with water, showed the two men that the paste could be modeled into the shape of the bowl, and, finally, pointed to himself. Then he took the bow and caressed it affectionately along its length: it was smooth, symmetrical, strong. He showed the two a bundle of long, straight branches that were lying a little distance away, and had them observe that the quality and the fiber of the wood were the same. He returned to the hut, and this time came out with two obsidian scrapers, one big and one small, and a rough block of obsidian.

The two observed him with curiosity and bewilderment. Achtiti picked up a flint stone, and showed them that, if he struck with precisely aimed small blows along particular contours of the block, it flaked cleanly, without breaking; in a few minutes of work, he had made a scraper, maybe still needing to be refined, but already usable. Then Achtiti took two branches, each a little less than a meter long, and began to scrape one of them. He worked with purpose and skill, in silence or humming, his mouth closed: after half an hour the branch was tapered at one end, and periodically Achtiti checked it, bending it over one knee to feel if it was flexible enough. Perhaps he perceived a trace of impatience in the attitude or comments of the two men, because he interrupted his work, went off among the huts, and returned accompanied by a boy. He entrusted the second branch and another scraper to him, and from then on they worked together. Indeed, the boy was as skillful as Achtiti; it was evident that for him, too, making a bow was not a new job. When the two branches were reduced to the right size and shape, Achtiti began to smooth them with a rough stone that to Wilkins appeared to be a fragment of a whetstone.

"He doesn't seem to be in a hurry," said Goldbaum.

"The Siriono are never in a hurry. Hurry is a sickness of ours," Wilkins answered.

"They have other sicknesses, however."

"Of course. But nowhere is it said that a civilization without sickness is possible."

"What do you suppose he wants from us?"

"I think I understand," Wilkins said. Achtiti continued to scrape the wood diligently, working around all sides and testing the surface with his fingers and his eyes, squinting, because he was a little farsighted. Finally, he tied the two untapered ends together, overlapping them for a short distance, and between the pointed ends he stretched a string of twisted gut: he had a certain air of pride, and showed the two that, if you pinched the string, it resonated for a long time, like a harp. He sent the boy to get an arrow, took aim, and shot: the arrow stuck quivering in the trunk of a palm fifty meters away. Then, with an emphatic gesture, he offered the bow to Wilkins, indicating with a nod that it was his: he should hold it, try it out. Then he took two matches from the open box, offered one to Wilkins and one to Goldbaum, squatted on the ground, wrapped his arms around his knees, and waited, but without impatience.

Goldbaum, with the match in his hand, was speechless. Then he said, "I think I understand, too."

"Yes," Wilkins answered. "As a lecture, it's clear enough: we wretched Siriono, if we don't have a scraper, we make one; and if we are without a bow, with the scraper we make the bow, and maybe we also make it smooth, because then it's a pleasure to look at and hold in your hand. You foreign sorcerers, who steal men's voices and put them in a box, you were left without matches: come on, make some."

"So?"

"We'll have to explain our limits." With two voices, or, rather, with four hands, they tried to convince Achtiti that although it's true that a match is small, much smaller than a bow (this was a point that Achtiti seemed to consider important), the head of the match contained an ingredient (how to explain it?) that dwelt far away, in the sun, in the depths of the earth, beyond the rivers and the forest. They were painfully conscious of the inadequacy of their defense: Achtiti stuck out his lips at them, shook his head, and said things to the boy that made him laugh.

"He must be telling him that we are bad sorcerers, scoundrels who only know how to talk big," said Goldbaum. Achtiti was a methodical man: he said something else to the boy, who grabbed the bow and some arrows and stood at a distance of twenty paces with a resolute air; he himself went off and returned with one of the knives found at the site of the base camp, which the fire had warped and severely oxidized. He picked up one of the watches off the ground and held it out to Wilkins. Wilkins, with the pale face of one who shows up unprepared for an important exam, made a sign of impotence. He opened the watchcase and showed Achtiti the minute gears, the thin balance wheel that never stopped, the tiny rubies, and then his own fingers: impossible! The same, or almost, happened with the tape recorder, which, however, Achtiti didn't want to touch: he made Wilkins pick it up himself, and stopped up his ears for fear of hearing his voice. And the knife? Achtiti seemed to want them to understand that it was a sort of makeup exam, that is, an elementary test, basic enough for any simpleton, sorcerer or no: go ahead, make a knife. A knife, look, isn't a kind of little beast with a beating heart, which is easy to kill but very difficult to bring back to life: it doesn't move, it doesn't make noise, and it's got only two parts—the Siriono themselves had three or four of them, which they had bought ten years earlier and had paid very little for, just an armful of papayas and two caiman skins.

"You answer—I've had enough." Goldbaum displayed less talent for mimickry and diplomacy than his colleague. He waved his arms vainly, in a gesture that not even Wilkins understood, and Achtiti, for the first time, burst into laughter; but it was not a reassuring laugh.

"What are you trying to tell him?"

"That perhaps we would manage to make a knife, but that we need some special rocks, rocks that burn and that aren't found in this country, plus time and a hot fire."

"I didn't understand, but he probably did. He was right to laugh: he must have thought that we just wanted to gain time until they come to get us. It's the number-one trick of all sorcerers and prophets."

Achtiti called out, and seven or eight robust warriors appeared. They seized the two men and shut them up in a hut of solid tree trunks. There were no openings; light entered only through the chinks in the roof. Goldbaum asked, "Do you think we'll be here long?" Wilkins answered, "I fear no; I hope yes."

But the Siriono are not a fierce people. They were content to leave them there to expiate their lies, providing them with plenty of water and a little food. For some obscure reason, perhaps because he felt offended, Achtiti no longer came to see them.

Goldbaum said, "I'm a good photographer, but without lenses and without film . . . Maybe I could make a camera obscura. What do you say?"

"That would amuse them. But they are asking us for something more: that we demonstrate, concretely, that our civilization is superior to theirs, that our sorcerers are more powerful than theirs."

"It's not as if I knew how to make many other things with my hands. I know how to drive a car. I also know how to change a light bulb or a fuse. Unclog a sink, sew on a button. But here there are neither sinks nor needles."

Wilkins meditated. "No," he said, "here it would take something more essential. If they let us out, I could try to take apart the magnetic tape recorder. How it's put together inside I don't know, but if there's a permanent magnet we're in business. We can make it float in a bowl of water and give them the compass, and at the same time show them the art of making a compass."

"Even though it's called a magnetic tape recorder, I don't think there are magnets inside," Goldbaum answered. "And

I'm not even sure that a compass would be very useful to the Siriono. For them the sun is enough: they aren't navigators, and when they set out into the forest they follow the marked trails."

"How do you make gunpowder? Maybe that's not too hard. Don't you just mix carbon, sulfur, and saltpeter?"

"Theoretically, yes. But where would you find saltpeter here, in the middle of the swamps? And there might be sulfur, but who knows where? And, finally, what use would gunpowder be, if they don't have an ordinary gun barrel?"

"I have an idea. People here can die as a result of a scratch, from septicemia or tetanus. We could ferment their grain, distill the infusion, and make alcohol for them; maybe they would also like to drink it, even if that's not exactly proper. They don't seem to be acquainted with either stimulants or depressants. It would be a fine bit of sorcery."

Goldbaum was tired. "We don't have a fermenting agent. I don't think I would be capable of recognizing one, and neither would you. And then I'd like to see you wrestling with the local potters to get them to build you a still. Maybe it's not completely impossible, but it's an undertaking that would require months, and we have only days."

It wasn't clear if the Siriono intended to make them die of starvation, or if they wished only to maintain them with the least expense while waiting for the boat to come up the river, or for the final, decisive idea to develop in the two men. Their days passed in a torpor that grew ever deeper, a waking sleep made up of damp heat, mosquitoes, hunger, and humiliation.

And yet both of them had studied for almost twenty years, knew many things about all human civilizations, ancient and modern, were interested in all primitive technologies, in Chaldean metallurgy, in Mycenean ceramics, in pre-Columbian weaving: and now perhaps (*perhaps!*) they would be able to split off a flint stone because Achtiti had taught them, while they were unable to teach Achtiti anything: only tell him by means of gestures about marvels that he didn't believe in, and show him miraculous things that they had brought with them, made by other hands, under another sky.

After almost a month of prison they were short of ideas, and felt worn down to a final impotence. The entire colossal edifice of modern technology was out of their reach: they had to confess to each other that not even one of the inventions of which their civilization was proud could be transmitted to the Siriono. They lacked the basic materials to start with, and, even if these could have been found nearby, the two Englishmen would have been unable to recognize or isolate them; none of the arts that they knew would be judged useful by the Siriono. If one of them had been good at drawing, they could have made a portrait of Achtiti, and, if nothing else, evoked wonder. If they had a year's time, they might perhaps convince their hosts of the usefulness of the alphabet, adapt it to their language, and teach Achtiti the art of writing. For several hours they discussed the idea of making soap for the Siriono: they could get potash from the wood ashes, and oil from the seeds of a local palm. But what use would soap be to the Siriono? They didn't have clothes, and it would not be easy to persuade them of the usefulness of washing themselves with soap.

Finally, they were reduced to a modest project: they would teach the Siriono to make candles. Modest but irreproachable; the Siriono had wax, wax from peccaries, which they used to grease their hair, and there was no difficulty about the wicks: they could use bristles from the same peccaries. The Siriono would appreciate the advantage of illuminating the inside of their huts at night. Of course, they might prefer to learn how to make a gun or an outboard motor: candles weren't much, but it was worth a try.

They were just attempting to get in touch with Achtiti, to negotiate their freedom in exchange for the candles, when they heard a big ruckus outside their prison. Soon afterward the door was opened, amid incomprehensible shouts, and Achtiti gestured to them to come out into the dazzling light of day: the boat had arrived.

The farewell was neither long nor ceremonious. Achtiti immediately stepped away from the prison door; he squatted on his heels, turning his back to them, and remained unmoving, as if turned to stone, while Siriono warriors led the two men to the bank of the river. Two or three women, laughing and shouting, exposed their stomachs in their direction; all the others in the village, even the children, swung their heads, singing "Luu, luu," and held out their hands, limp and as if detached, letting them dangle from their wrists like overripe fruit.

Wilkins and Goldbaum had no baggage. They got into the

boat, which was piloted by Suarez himself, and begged him to leave as quickly as possible.

THE SIRIONO are not invented. They actually exist, or at least they did until around 1945, but what one knows of them makes one think that, at least as a people, they will not survive for long. They were described by Allan R. Holmberg in a recent monograph ("The Siriono of Eastern Bolivia"): they lead a subsistence-level existence, which alternates between nomadism and primitive agriculture. They are not familiar with metals, they do not possess terms for numbers higher than three, and, although they often have to cross swamps and rivers, they do not know how to build boats. They do know, however, that at one time they were able to do so, and the story is passed down among them of a hero who had the name of the Moon, and who had taught their people (then much more numerous) three arts: to light fires, to carve out canoes, and to make bows. Of these, only the last survives; they have forgotten even the method of making fire. They told Holmberg that in a time not too far back (two, three generations ago: around the time when among us the first internal combustion engines were invented, electric light became widespread, and the complex structure of the atom was beginning to be understood) some of them knew how to make fire by twirling a stick in a hole in a piece of wood. But at that time the Siriono lived in another land, with a desert-like climate, where it was easy to find dry wood and tinder. Now they live among swamps and forests, in perpetual dampness. Since they could no longer find dry wood, the method of the stick in the hole could no longer be practiced, and was forgotten.

Fire itself, however, they kept. In each of their villages or wandering bands there is at least one old woman whose job it is to maintain a live spark in a brazier of tufo. This art is not so difficult as that of lighting a fire by means of rubbing sticks, but it's not elementary, either: especially in the rainy season, the flame has to be fed palm flowers, which are dried in the heat of that flame. These old vestals are very diligent, because if their fire dies they are put to death: not as punishment but because they are judged to be useless. All the Siriono who are judged to be useless because they are incapable of hunting, sowing, and plowing with a wooden plow are left to die. A Siriono is old at forty.

I repeat, they are not invented. They were reported by *Scientific American* in October, 1969, and they have a sinister renown: they teach us that not in every place and not in every era is humanity destined to advance.

Bureau of Vital Statistics

There were four elevators, but one, as usual, was out of service. It wasn't always the same one and even the sign hanging on the door wasn't always the same. This one, for instance, said "Out of Service"; others might say "Not Working" or "Broken" or "Don't Touch" or even "Back Soon." Maybe it was the doorman, or the superintendent, who changed the signs according to some vaguely ironic whim. There were lines in front of the three other elevators, and this, too, happened every day, at the beginning and at the end of the workday. If his office hadn't been on the ninth floor, Arrigo would have taken the stairs; sometimes he did anyway, for the exercise, but that morning he felt a little tired.

The elevator finally arrived, and it was already full of employees coming from the basement and the sub-basement. Arrigo made his way in energetically but without shoving.

The elevator rose, stopping with a jerk at every floor, and people got on and off, greeting each other distractedly. On the ninth floor, Arrigo himself got off and punched his time card. For two years now there had been a time clock on every floor. It had been a sensible innovation. Previously, there had been only one, on the ground floor, which always caused a terrible bottleneck, partly because there was little discipline, and people tried to push in front of you. In the office, people were already at their desks. Arrigo sat at his post, pulled the color photograph of his wife and their little girl out of the top drawer, and from the second drawer took writing supplies and the index cards left over from the previous day. This was the result of one of the boss's obsessions: at the end of the day, all the desks had to be cleared. Who knows why, certainly not for cleaning, because the desks were cleaned only two or three times a year: if you didn't want dust on your desk, you had to clean it yourself.

Arrigo's job was administrative in nature. Every day, he received a packet of index cards from the floor above. Each card contained the name of a human being and the date of his or her death; Arrigo had only to specify the cause. He would often get angry, for various reasons. The expiration date wasn't always the same: it could be years ahead, or months or days, for no apparent reason, and he felt that this was an injustice. Nor did it seem reasonable that there were no rules regarding age: some days he was handed hundreds of cards for newborns. Then, the boss complained if Arrigo kept to generic formulas: the man must be a sadist or a fan of

crime news. It wasn't enough for Arrigo to write "accident."
He wanted all the details and was never satisfied. He always
demanded a correlation between the data on the cards and
the cause of death, and this often embarrassed Arrigo.

The first index card of the day wasn't a problem. It bore
the name of Yen Ch'ing-Hsu, fifty-eight years old, single,
born in Han Tou, where he still resided, dockworker, no illnesses to speak of. Arrigo had no idea where Han Tou was: if
he were to check the atlas every time, he'd never get anything
done. Yen still had thirty-six days to live and Arrigo imagined
him against the backdrop of an exotic sunset, sitting on a roll
of cable before a turbid sea the color of a ripe banana; he was
exhausted by his daily work, sad and alone. A man like this
doesn't fear death and doesn't seek it, either, but he may act
carelessly. Arrigo thought about it for a moment and then had
him fall from a scaffold: he wouldn't suffer much.

PEDRO GONZALES de Eslava didn't give him much trouble,
either. In spite of the pompous name, he must have been a
poor devil—he drank, had been involved in many fights
among illegal immigrants, was forty-six years old, and had
worked on half a dozen farms in the far south. He had five
more months and would leave behind four children, who,
however, lived with his wife and not with him. The wife was
Puerto Rican, like Pedro; she was young, and she also
worked. Arrigo consulted the medical encyclopedia and
came up with hepatitis.

He was studying the third index card when Fernanda called him on the phone. She had seen in the paper that *Metropolis* was playing at some art house cinema; why not go see it tonight? Arrigo didn't like being interrupted at work and was noncommittal. The third index card was fairly obvious; everyone knows what happens to a man who races motorbikes. No one was forcing him to do it; he had only to choose a different profession—in cases like this, there's no need to have scruples. But he felt obliged to provide the details of the fatal accident and the hospital record.

He had no sympathy for Pierre-Jean La Motte. He was born in Lyons, but at the age of thirty-two he was already a full professor of political science at the University of Rio: evidently he was a man with connections. He had only twenty days to live, though he was in excellent health and played tennis every morning. Arrigo was racking his brains for an appropriate cause of death for La Motte when Lorusso came by and invited him to go for coffee. Arrigo went down with him to the vending machines on the fourth floor. Lorusso was dull. He had a son who wasn't doing well in math, and Arrigo thought that, with a father like that, it would be surprising if the son were a prodigy. Then Lorusso started to complain about his wife, who spent too much money, and about the heat that didn't work.

The coffee machine didn't work well, either. Lorusso banged on it and at long last it spat out two cups of coffee, pale and insipid but boiling hot. As Arrigo forced himself to gulp down the coffee, scalding his throat, Lorusso talked on about the paycheck that always came late and the deductions that were always too high. Finally, back at his desk, Arrigo squashed Pierre-Jean like a worm: brain hemorrhage—that'll teach him.

At around ten, Arrigo was finished with the cards left over from the previous day, but the office boy had already put the new cards on his desk. The first was all crumpled, maybe by the dating machine: he could make out only that it was for a person of the female sex, by the name of Adelia. Arrigo put the card aside, so much the better for Adelia: it's always useful to gain time. At any rate, he might decide to write a report: more and more often it happens that the first card of each packet is damaged . . . a regrettable occurrence . . . will maintenance please take care of it . . . sincerely yours. Instead he paused over the next card. Karen Kvarna, aged eight, born in Slidre, a mountain village in the heart of Norway. Karen, only child, illnesses N.A. (not available), student, was to die the following day. Arrigo was stuck. He imagined her flaxen-haired, kind, cheerful, serene, against the backdrop of solemn, immaculate mountains: if she had to die, then it would be without him, he would not take part in this. He grabbed the card and knocked on the boss's door: he heard a grumbled "Come in," entered, and said that it was a disgrace. That the work was poorly organized, that the purchase of the random-izer had been an idiotic idea, that the cards were full of mistakes—for example, this one right here. That they were all sheep and careerists and no one dared protest and no one took the job seriously. That he had had enough, that he couldn't care less about promotion, and that he wanted to be transferred.

The boss must have been expecting a scene from Arrigo for quite a while, because he gave no sign of surprise or indignation. Perhaps he was even glad to be rid of a pro-grammer with such an unstable character. He told Arrigo to stop by again the next day. And the next day he gave him his transfer orders and made him sign two or three explanatory documents. Thus Arrigo found himself demoted from grade 7 to grade 6 and transferred to a small office in the attic of the building, in charge of determining the shape of the noses of newborns.

The Girl in the Book

Umberto was not so young anymore. He had some trouble with his lungs, and the doctor had sent him to the seaside for a month. It was the month of October, and Umberto hated the sea; he hated the in-between seasons, solitude, and, above all, illness. So he was in a vile mood, and it seemed to him that he would never get better, that in fact his illness would get worse, and he would die there, on sick leave, among people he didn't know—die of dampness, of boredom, and of the sea air. But he was an obedient man, who stayed where he was put; if he had been sent to the seaside, it was a sign that he ought to be there. Every so often he took the train and returned to town to spend the night with Eva, but he left again the next morning, sadly, because it seemed to him that Eva was doing fine without him.

PRIMO LEVI

When one is used to working, it's painful to waste time, and in order not to waste too much time, or not to feel that he was wasting it, Umberto took long walks beside the sea and through the hills. Taking a walk is not like taking a trip: on a trip you make grand discoveries; on a walk you may make many discoveries, but they are small. Tiny green crabs wandered about the cliffs, not walking backward, as they are said to, but, rather, sideways, in a comical manner: endearing, but Umberto would rather have cut off a finger than touch one. Abandoned mill wheels, around them still visible the circular track where the mule had walked, who knows how many years earlier and for how many years. Two extraordinary inns, where you could get wine and homemade pasta that you wouldn't dream of in Milan. But the most curious discovery was La Bomboniera.

La Bomboniera was a tiny white square two-story villa, perched on a rise. It did not have a front, or, rather, it had four, all identical, each with a door of polished wood and with intricate decorations and plasterwork in an Art Deco style. The four corners were topped by graceful little turrets that had the shape of tulips but in fact were bathrooms; this was indicated by four ceramic pipes that, crudely set into the walls, descended to the ground. The windows of the villa were always darkened by black-painted shutters, and the plate on the gate bore an impossible name: Harmonika Grinkiavicius. The plate itself was odd, too: the exotic name was surrounded by a triple ellipse, on which, from the outside in, were the colors yellow, green, and red in sequence. It was the only note of color against the white plaster of the villa.

Almost without realizing it, Umberto got in the habit of passing La Bomboniera every day. It wasn't uninhabited: an old woman lived there, occasionally visible, who was neat and spare, with hair as white as the villa and a face slightly too red. Signora Grinkiavicius went out once a day, always at the same time, whatever the weather, but for just a few minutes. She had well-made but old-fashioned clothes, an umbrella, a wide-brimmed straw hat with a black velvet ribbon that tied under her chin. She walked with small, decisive steps, as if she were in a hurry to reach some destination, yet she always took the same route, returned home, and immediately closed the door behind her. She never appeared at the windows.

From the shopkeepers he couldn't get much information. Yes, the woman was a foreigner, a widow for at least thirty years, educated, wealthy. She did many charitable deeds. She smiled at everyone but spoke to no one. She went to Mass on Sunday morning. She had never been to the doctor or even to the pharmacist. Her husband had bought the villa, but no one remembered anything about him anymore—maybe he hadn't even really been her husband. Umberto was curious, and, besides, he suffered from his solitude; one day he got up his courage and stopped the woman, on the pretext of asking her where a certain street was. She answered in a few words, precisely and in good Italian. After that Umberto couldn't think up any other ploys with which to start a conversation. He confined himself to plotting so as to run into her on his morning round and greet her; she responded with a smile. Umberto recovered and returned to Milan.

Umberto liked to read. He came across a book that appealed
to him: it was the memoir of an English soldier who had
fought against the Italians in Cyrenaica, had been taken pris-
oner and interned near Pavia, but then had escaped and joined
the partisans. He hadn't been a great partisan; he liked girls better than guns, and described several slight, happy love affairs,
and a longer, stormier one, with a Lithuanian refugee. In this
episode the Englishman's story proceeded from a walk to a trot
and then a gallop: against the tense, dark background of the
German occupation and the Allied bombardments, he depicted
wild bicycle flights on shadowy roads, in defiance of patrols
and curfew, and daring adventures in the underground of
smuggling and the black market. A memorable portrait of the
Lithuanian emerged: tireless and indestructible, a good shot
when necessary, extraordinarily vital: a Diana-Minerva grafted
onto the opulent body (described in detail by the Englishman)
of a Juno. The two possessed souls got lost and found in the valleys of the Apennines, impatient with discipline, today partisans, tomorrow deserters, then partisans again; they consumed
dinners in huts and caves at dizzying heights, followed by
heroic nights. The Lithuanian was depicted as a lover without
equal, impetuous and refined, never distracted: polyglot and
polyvalent, she knew how to love in her own language, in Italian, in English, in Russian, in German, and in at least two others, which the author skipped over. This torrential love affair
rolled on for thirty pages before the Englishman troubled to
reveal the name of his Amazon: on the thirty-first he remembered, and the name was Harmonika.

Umberto started and closed the book. The name could be a random coincidence, but that odd surname and the colored circles that surrounded it returned to the screen of his memory; the colors must have a meaning. In vain he looked through the house for some reference book. The next evening, he went to the library, and found what he wanted to know: the flag of the short-lived Lithuanian Republic, between the two world wars, was yellow, green, and red. Not only that: under "Lithuania" in the encyclopedia his eye fell on Basanavicius, the founder of the first newspaper in the Lithuanian language; on Slezavicius, Prime Minister in the twenties; on Stanevicius, an eighteenth-century poet* (where does one not find an eighteenth-century poet!); and on Neveravicius the novelist. Was it possible? Possible that the taciturn benefactress and the bacchant were the same person?

From that moment on Umberto could think only of finding a pretext for returning to the seaside, going so far as to hope for a mild recurrence of his pleurisy; he couldn't come up with anything plausible, but he made up some nonsense for Eva and went off one Saturday, taking the book. He felt cheerful and intent, like a hound on the trail of a fox; he marched from the station to La Bomboniera at a military clip, rang the bell without hesitation, and immediately launched into his subject, with a half lie fabricated on the spot. He lived in Milan but was from Val Tidone: he had heard that the signora knew that area, he felt nostalgic, and would love to

* Actually, Stanevicius lived from 1799 to 1848.

talk with her about it. Signora Grinkavicius looked better when viewed close up; her face was wrinkled but fresh and well modeled, and a laughing light shone in her eyes. Yes, she had been there, many years before; but he, where had he heard all that?

Umberto counterattacked: "You are Lithuanian, right?"

"I was born there. It's an unhappy land. But I studied elsewhere, in different places."

"So you speak many languages?"

The woman was now visibly on the defensive, and she turned obstinate: "I asked you a question, and you answer me with another question. I want to know where you heard about my affairs. That's legitimate, don't you think?"

"From this book," Umberto answered.

"Give it to me!"

Umberto attempted a parry and retreat, but with little conviction. He realized at that moment that the true purpose of his return to the coast was precisely that: to see Harmonika in the act of reading the adventures of Harmonika. The woman grabbed the volume, sat down beside the window, and became engrossed in her reading. Umberto, although he had not been asked, sat down, too. He saw on Harmonika's face—still youthful but red because of all the burst capillaries—the movements of the soul pass like the shadows of clouds on a plain swept by the wind: regret, amusement, irritation, and other, less decipherable sensations. She read for half an hour, then without speaking held the book out to him.

"Is it true?" Umberto asked. The woman was silent for so long that Umberto feared she was offended; but she smiled and answered:

"Look at me. More than thirty years have passed, and I am different. Memory, too, is different. It's not true that memories stay fixed in the mind, frozen: they, too, go astray, like the body. Yes, I remember a time when I was different. I would like to be the girl in the book: I would be happy also just to have been her, but I never was. It wasn't I who attracted the Englishman. I remember that I was malleable, like clay in his hands. My love affairs . . . that's what interests you, right? Well, they are fine where they are: in my memory, faded, withered, with a trace of perfume, like a collection of dried flowers. In yours they have become shiny and bright like plastic toys. I don't know which are more beautiful. You choose. Come, take your book and go back to Milan."

Buffet Dinner

Immediately upon entering through the front door, Innaminka felt uneasy and regretted having accepted the invitation. There was a butler of sorts, with a green sash around his belly, who took people's coats. Innaminka, whose coat was part of his body, shivered and felt dizzy at the thought that someone might take it from him. But there was more: behind the butler rose a great spiral staircase of beautiful polished black wood, broad and majestic but unmanageable. Unmanageable for him, that is. The other guests mounted it with ease, while he didn't dare even try. He kept turning in circles, embarrassed, waiting till no one was looking. On level ground he was good, but the length of his hindquarters alone was an obstacle—his feet were more or less twice as long as the stairs were deep. He waited a little more, sniffing at the walls and trying to appear indifferent, and once everyone else was upstairs he endeavored to go up as well.

He tried different methods: grabbing the banister with his front legs, or bending over and trying to climb on all fours, even employing his tail—but actually it was the tail, more than anything else, that got in the way. He ended up climbing clumsily sideways, placing his feet lengthwise on each step, his tail folded ignobly over his back. It took him a full ten minutes.

Upstairs was a long, narrow room, with a table placed crosswise; there were paintings on the walls, some depicting human or animal forms, others depicting nothing. Along the walls, and scattered around the floor, were bronze or marble figures that Innaminka found pleasing and vaguely familiar. The room was already crowded, but more people kept arriving: the men were in evening attire, the women wore long black dresses and were bedecked with jewels, their eyelids painted green or blue. Innaminka hesitated for a moment and then, sidling along the wall and avoiding abrupt movements, took refuge in a corner. The other guests looked at him with mild curiosity. In passing, he overheard a few casual comments: "He's pretty, isn't he?" ". . . no, he doesn't have one, dear. Can't you see he's a male?" "I heard on TV that they are almost extinct. . . . No, not for the fur, which isn't worth much anyway. It's because they destroy the crops."

AFTER A WHILE, the young hostess emerged from a group of guests and came toward him. She was very thin, with large, wide-set gray eyes and an expression between annoyance and surprise, as if someone had brusquely woken her up at that very moment. She told him that she had heard a lot about him, and this Innaminka found hard to believe: maybe it was just a form of greeting, and she said it to all her guests. She asked him if he'd like something to eat or drink: she didn't seem very intelligent, but she probably had a kind heart, and it was precisely because of her kindness rather than her intelligence that she realized that Innaminka understood her fairly well but could not answer her, and she moved on.

Actually, Innaminka was hungry and thirsty: not to an unbearable degree, but enough to make him uncomfortable. Now, the dinner was one of those melancholy buffet affairs, where you have to choose what you want from a distance, craning between heads and shoulders, find the plates, find the silverware and the paper napkins, get in line, reach the table, serve yourself, and then back away, making sure not to spill anything, either on yourself or on anyone else. Besides, he could see neither grass nor hay on the table: there was a rather appetizing-looking salad, and peas in a brown sauce, but as Innaminka hesitated, debating whether or not to get in line, the one dish and then the other were finished. Innaminka gave up. He turned his back on the table and, proceeding with care through the crowd, tried to return to his corner. He thought with loving nostalgia of his wife, and of his youngest, who was growing up: he was a good jumper and went out to pasture by himself, but now and then he still demanded to return to his mother's pouch—indeed, he was a little spoiled, and liked to spend the night in that warm darkness.

During his laborious retreat, he encountered several wait-
ers who carried trays and offered glasses of wine and
orangeade and canapés that looked tempting. He didn't even
think about taking a glass in the middle of the crowd, while
everyone was bumping into him. He gathered up his courage,
grabbed a canapé, and brought it to his mouth, but it instantly
fell apart in his fingers, so that he had to lick them one by
one and then lick his lips and whiskers for a long time. He
looked around, suspicious, but no, no one was paying any
attention. He crouched in his corner, and to pass the time he
began to observe the guests closely, trying to imagine how
they would behave, men and women, if they were being
chased by a dog. No mistaking it—in those long wide skirts,
the women would never get off the ground, and even the
swiftest among the men, even with a good running start,
wouldn't be able to jump a third of the distance that he could
jump from a standstill. But you can never tell, maybe they
were good at other things.

HE WAS hot and thirsty, and at some point he realized with
dismay that an increasingly urgent need was growing in him.
He thought that it surely must happen to others, too, and for
a few minutes he looked around to see how they dealt with
it, but it seemed that no one else had his problem. So very
slowly he approached a large pot in which a ficus tree grew,
and pretending to sniff the leaves he sat astride the pot and
relieved himself. The leaves were fresh and shiny and had a

nice smell. Innaminka ate a couple and found them tasty but had to stop because he noticed a woman staring at him.

She stared at him and came closer. Innaminka realized that it was too late to pretend that nothing had happened and move away. She was young and had broad shoulders, massive bones, strong hands, a pale face, and clear eyes. To Innaminka, of course, her feet were of primary importance, but the woman's skirt was so long and her shoes so complicated that he couldn't get even an idea of their shape and length. For a moment he feared that the woman had noticed the business with the ficus tree and had come to reprimand him or punish him, but he soon realized that it wasn't so. She sat down on a small armchair beside him and started talking to him sweetly. Innaminka understood hardly anything she said, but at once he felt calmer; he lowered his ears and made himself more comfortable. The woman came even closer and began to caress him, first on the neck and back, then, seeing that he was closing his eyes, under his chin and on his chest, between his front paws, where there is that triangle of white fur that kangaroos are so proud of.

The woman talked and talked, in a subdued tone, as if she were afraid the others would hear. Innaminka understood that she was unhappy, that someone had behaved badly toward her, that this someone was, or had been, her man, that this event had occurred a short time ago, perhaps that very evening: but nothing more than that. Since he, too, was unhappy, he felt sympathetic toward the woman, and for the first time that evening he stopped wishing that the reception would soon be over; instead he hoped that the woman would continue to caress him and, in particular, that her hands would go lower and run lightly and knowingly along the mighty muscles of his tail and his thighs, of which he was even prouder than of his white triangle.

This, however, was not to be. The woman continued to caress him, but with increasing distraction, paying no attention to his shivers of pleasure, and continuing all the while to complain about certain human troubles of hers that seemed to Innaminka not to amount to much—to one man instead of another man whom she would have preferred. Innaminka thought that, if this was how things stood, the woman would do better to caress this second man instead of him; and that maybe that was exactly what she was doing; and furthermore that she was beginning to bore him, given that for at least a quarter of an hour she had been repeating the same caresses and the same words. In short, it was clear that she was thinking of herself and not of him.

Suddenly a man sprang out of the seething crowd, grabbed the woman's wrist, jerked her to her feet, and said something very unpleasant and brutal to her. He then dragged her away and she followed, without giving Innaminka so much as a farewell glance.

Innaminka had had enough. From his observation post he stretched up as high as he could, straightening his back and raising himself on his hind legs and tail as on a tripod, to see if anyone was starting to leave. He didn't want to attract attention by being the first. But as soon as he caught sight of an elegant elderly couple making the rounds to say their goodbyes and heading toward the cloakroom, Innaminka took off.

He negotiated the first few meters slinking between the legs of the guests, below the level of breasts and stomachs; he stayed low, supported alternately on his hind legs and on his front legs with the help of his tail. But when he was near the table, which by now had been cleared, he noticed that the floor on either side of the table was clear, too, and so he jumped right over it, feeling his lungs fill effortlessly with air and with joy. With a second leap he was at the head of the stairs: rushing, he miscalculated the distance and landed off-balance on the top steps. There was nothing for it but to descend that way, like a sack, half crawling and half rolling. But as soon as he reached the ground floor he hopped to his feet. Under the expressionless gaze of the doorman, he took a deep, voluptuous breath of the damp, grimy night air and immediately set off along Via Borgospesso, no longer in a rush, with long, happy, elastic leaps.

The TV Fans from Delta Cep.

Dear Piero Bianucci,[*]

You will be surprised to receive a letter from an admirer, so quickly and from so far away. We know your silly notions about the speed of light; where we are, a modest one-time supplement to the TV subscription fee is all it takes to be able to send and receive intergalactic messages in real time, or almost. As for me, I am a great admirer of your TV programs, and especially of the ad for tomato puree. I wanted to tell you that I was very enthusiastic about your program last Tuesday, where you spoke about the Cepheids. In fact, I was pleased to learn that you call us that, because our sun is indeed a Cepheid; I mean, it's a star much bigger than

[*] Editor-in-chief of the newspaper *La Stampa*, author of numerous popular science books, and creator and director of a science program on Italian TV.

yours, and it pulsates regularly, with a period of five days and nine hours, earth time. It is, to be precise, the Cepheid of Cepheus—what a coincidence! But before I embark on describing our *way of life*★ I want to tell you that my girlfriends and I really like your beard. The men here don't have beards—in fact, they don't even have heads. Our men are ten or twelve centimeters long and look like your asparagus, and when we want to be inseminated we put them under our armpits for two or three minutes, as you do with thermometers when you take your temperature. We have ten armpits: we are all built with binary symmetry, so that our width is the golden section of our radius. This is unique in our galaxy, and we're very proud of it. Males cost from twenty to fifty thousand lire depending on their age and condition, and they don't bother us much.

By the way, don't get your hopes up: our temperature varies, around -20° C in winter, 110° C in summer— but we'll become friends anyway. I heard that you are an astrophile, and this made me . . . [*indecipherable*] because my friends and I also spend many evenings in the posterior hemisphere contemplating the starry sky; we enjoyed locating your sun, which, seen from here, is a little shy of the seventh magnitude and lies in a constellation we call Jadikus (it's a kitchen utensil). Almost all of us, except for a few who love solitude, live in the

★ In English in the original.

anterior hemisphere, because it has more light and a better view. After all, our planet isn't big: changing hemispheres is a short trip of three or four kilometers that can be made on foot, or by swimming in the rivers when they're not frozen or dry.

We are also far from our sun, so it's rare for the rocks to melt, except for sulfur. When I spoke of summer and winter, I was referring to the pulsations of our sun. It wouldn't be easy for you people to adapt. There is a law-enforcement agency for the distracted and for the habitually late; sirens blare in all the towns and villages, and we have to burrow underground within half an hour. Each of us takes along her males. They say it's quite a spectacle, but only the girls from law enforcement can see it, with periscopes, from inside their adiabatic observatories: apparently the sun swells before your very eyes, and in a few minutes the sea starts to boil. It's a sea of water and sulfur dioxide, with iron salts—aluminum, titanium, and manganese—dissolved in it. We also have an armor made of iron oxide and manganese, and we change it when it gets too tight. We never go into the sea, because we are alkaline and the water is acid and would dissolve us. That happens sometimes: those who are tired of life throw themselves deliberately into the sea. It's not a very deep sea, and when the sun swells it evaporates in a few hours; it turns into an ugly expanse of gray and brown salt and all the water goes up into the sky to form a mist over the sun.

The summer lasts two of your days; we spend it sleeping and laying eggs. Our optimal temperature is around 46° C, so that if you and I were to meet during the pleasant season we could even touch; I'd like that, but it probably won't happen because . . . [*indecipherable*] aren't here yet. Then the heat gradually subsides, rain pours down, hot and then warm, and the grass starts to sprout again. It's the season when we all go out to pasture and exchange news. Last fall one of my friends told me that she saw a supernova; there hadn't been one in a while and she urged me to let you know about it. From your perspective, it should be in the neighborhood of Scorpio; if you pay the one-time tachyonic subscription you can see it in ten days, otherwise you'll have to wait 3,485 years.

At the end of autumn, everything freezes: the sea with all its salts, the grass trapped in the rain and the dew, as well as everyone who remains outside. Winter is pleasant: our caves are well heated, we eat canned food, we get inseminated three or four times by various males, to set ourselves apart a little, but also because it's fashionable; we make music with our stridulating organs, watch all the TV in the universe, and organize literary prizes. Three years ago I even won a prize. It was for a very sexy short story, about a girl who had bought a male with her first paycheck and then she fell for him and didn't want to exchange him or have him pulped. I wrote it in 2 and 36 hundredths seconds. We do everything pretty quickly.

Your TV show is one of the most popular, especially because of the purees, which are of great interest to us. If you are able to submit your one-time payment and respond in a reasonable time, please send me the formula for your most important: (a) anti-fermentatives; (b) anti-parasitics; (c) anti-conceptions;★ (d) anti-aesthetics; (e) anti-Semitics; (f) antipyretics; (g) antiquarians; (h) antihelminthics; (i) antiphons; (j) antitheses; (k) antelopes.

As a matter of fact, we of the eighth planet of Delta Cepheid are also exposed to many dangers and threats from which we need to protect ourselves. In particular, regarding points c and h there was much discussion in my den last winter, because the TV commercials weren't clear. At any rate, my friends and I would like to get the local chemical industry to produce them so we can try them—we had the impression that they could provide relief for some of our ills.

Cordially yours, . . . [*signature illegible*] and friends
Delta Cep./8, d.3° a.3,576.10^{-11}
Translated by Primo Levi.

★ In Italian, the word contraceptive is *anticoncezionale*.

The Molecule's Defiance

I've had it," he said to me. "I need a change. I'll quit, find some ordinary job, maybe unloading stuff at the whole-sale market. Or I'll leave, go away—on the road, you spend less than you do at home, and you can always find some way of earning money. But I am not ever going to the factory again."

I told Rinaldo to think it over, that it's never a good idea to make a decision in the heat of the moment, that a factory job isn't something to throw away, and that in any case it would be better if he told me the story from the beginning. He is enrolled in the university, but he does shifts at the factory. Shift work is unpleasant—every week your schedule changes, and the rhythm of your life, too, so you have to get used to not getting used to things. In general, middle-aged people manage this better than the young.

"No, it's not a question of shifts. It's that a batch spoiled on me. Eight tons to throw away."

A batch that spoils is one that solidifies halfway through the preparation: the liquid becomes gelatinous, or even hard, like horn. It's a phenomenon that is called by fancy names like gelatinization or premature polymerization, but it's a traumatic event, an ugly sight, not to mention the money that's lost. It shouldn't happen, but sometimes it does happen, even if you're paying attention, and when it happens it leaves its mark. I told Rinaldo that it's useless to cry over spilled milk, and immediately I regretted it—it wasn't the right thing to say. But what can you say to a decent person who has made a mistake, who doesn't know how he did it, and who carries his guilt like a load of lead? The only thing to do is offer him a cognac and invite him to talk.

"It's not because of the boss, you see, or even the owner. It's the thing in itself, and the way it happened. It was a simple procedure, I had already done it at least thirty times, so that I knew the formula by heart and didn't even have to look at it . . ."

I, too, have had batches spoil in the course of my career, so I know very well what it's like. I asked him, "Isn't it possible that's the problem, the cause of the trouble? You thought you knew it all by heart, but you forgot some detail, or made a mistake in a temperature, or added something you weren't supposed to?"

"No. I checked afterward, and everything was normal. Now the lab is working on it, trying to figure it out. I'm the accused, but still if I made a mistake I'd like to find out. I really would. I'd prefer if someone said to me, 'You idiot, you did this and that which you shouldn't have done,' rather than sit here asking myself questions. And then it's lucky that no one died—no one was even hurt—and the reactor shaft didn't get bent. There's only the financial damage, and if I had the money, I swear, I would happily pay.

"So. I had the morning shift. I had come on duty at six, and everything was in order. Before going off, Morra left me the instructions. Morra is an old guy, who worked his way up; he left me the production note with all the materials checked off at the right times, the cards for the automatic scale, so there was nothing out of the ordinary—he is certainly not the type to leave a mess, and he had no reason to, because everything was going well. Day was just breaking: you could see the mountains, almost close enough to touch. I glanced at the thermograph, which was functioning properly; there was even a bump on the curve at four in the morning, registering fifteen degrees higher. It's a bump that appears every day, always at the same time, and neither the engineer nor the electrician has ever understood why—as if it had taken up the habit of telling a lie every day, and, just as with liars, after a while no one pays attention anymore. I also glanced inside the reactor through the spy hole: there was no smoke, there was no foam, the mixture was beautifully transparent and circulating as smoothly as water. It wasn't water; it was a synthetic resin, of the type that is formulated to harden, but only later, in the molds.

"Anyway, I was feeling calm, there was no reason to worry. I still had two hours to wait before starting the tests, and I confess that I had other things on my mind. I was thinking . . . well, yes, I was thinking about the chaos of atoms and molecules inside that reactor, as if every molecule were standing there with its hands outstretched, ready to grasp the hand of the molecule passing by to form a chain. There came to mind those great men who had guessed the existence of atoms from common sense, reasoning on matter and void, two thousand years before we appeared with our equipment to prove them right. And—because when we were camping this summer my girl made me read Lucretius—I also remembered *Corpora constabunt ex partibus infinitis,*★ and the guy who said 'Everything flows.' From time to time, I looked through the spy hole, and it seemed to me that I could see them, all those molecules buzzing like bees around a hive.

"So, everything was flowing and I had every reason to be calm, although I hadn't forgotten what they teach you when you're entrusted with a reactor. And that is, that everything is fine as long as one molecule connects to another as if each had only two hands: they're not supposed to make more than a chain, or a rosary of molecules—it can be long, but only a chain. And you have to keep in mind that, among the many molecules, some have three hands, and there's the rub. In fact, they are inserted on purpose: the third hand is the one that is supposed to catch hold later—when *we* decide, not when

★ De Rerum Natura I: 615: "[the smallest] bodies will be composed of infinite particles."

they do. If the third hands grip too soon, every rosary joins with two or three other rosaries, and in the end they've formed a single molecule, a monster molecule as big as the whole reactor, and then you're in a fix. Goodbye to 'Everything flows'—nothing flows, everything is blocked and there is nothing to be done about it."

I was observing him as he talked, and I refrained from interrupting him, although he was telling me things I already know. Talking was doing him good: his eyes shone, perhaps partly because of the cognac, but he was calming down. Talking is the best medicine.

"Well, as I was saying, every so often I glanced at the mixture, and I was thinking about the things I was telling you, and also about others that had nothing to do with this. The motors were humming calmly, the cam was rotating slowly, and the needle of the thermograph was drawing on its face an outline that corresponded to the movement of the cam. Inside the reactor the agitator was turning regularly and you could see that the resin was slowly becoming thicker. Already around seven it was beginning to stick to the walls and make little bubbles: this is a sign that I discovered, and I also taught it to Morra and the guy on the third shift—it's always someone different, so I don't even know his name. Anyway, it's a sign that the heating is almost done, and that it's time to take the first sample and test the viscosity.

"I went down to the floor below, because an eight-thousand-liter reactor isn't a toy, and it sits a good two meters below the floor; and while I was there, fooling with the discharge valve, I heard the motor of the agitator change tone. It changed just a little, maybe not even by a sharp, but this is a sign, too, and not a good one. I threw away the sample and everything, and in an instant I was upstairs with my eye glued to the spy hole, and it was a really hideous sight. The whole scene had changed: the blades of the agitator were slicing a mass that looked like polenta, and was rising right before my eyes. I stopped the agitator, since by now it was useless, and stood there as if spellbound, with my knees shaking. What to do? It was too late to unload the mixture, or to call the doctor, who at that hour was still in bed: and besides, when a batch spoils it's as if somebody had died: the best remedies come to mind afterward.

"A mass of foam was rising, slowly but relentlessly. Coming to the surface were bubbles as big as a man's head but not round: deformed, in all shapes, with the walls striped as if with nerves and veins; they burst and immediately others appeared, but it wasn't like beer, where the foam subsides, and rarely overflows the glass. This mass kept rising. I called, and several people came, including the head of the department, and they all said what they thought but no one knew what to do, and meanwhile the foam was only half a meter below the spy hole. Every time a bubble burst, bits of spit flew out and stuck under the glass of the spy hole and smeared it; soon you wouldn't be able to see anything. By now it was clear that the foam wasn't going to subside: it would keep rising until it clogged all the cooling pipes, and then goodbye.

"With the agitator off, it was quiet, and you could hear a

PRIMO LEVI

growing noise, as in science-fiction films when something horrible is about to happen: a murmur and a rumbling that kept getting louder, like an upset stomach. It was my eight-cubic-meter molecule, with the gas trapped inside it, all the gas that couldn't get out, that wanted to emerge, give birth to itself. I could neither run away nor stand there and wait: I was terrified, but I also felt responsible, the mixture was mine. By now the spy hole was blocked, all you could see was a reddish glow. I don't know if what I did was right or wrong: I was afraid that the reactor would burst, and so I took the wrench and removed all the bolts on the hatch.

"The hatch rose by itself, not suddenly but gently, solemnly, as when tombs open and the dead arise. A slow thick stream came out, disgusting, a yellow mass full of lumps and nodules. We all jumped back, but it cooled right away on the floor, as if it had sat down, and you could see that the volume wasn't so great after all. Inside the reactor the foam subsided about half a meter, then stopped and gradually hardened. So the show is over; we looked at each other and our faces were not a pretty sight. Mine must have been the ugliest of all, but there were no mirrors."

I tried to calm Rinaldo, or at least distract him, but I'm afraid I didn't succeed, and for a good reason. Among all my experiences of work, none is so alien and inimical as that of a batch that spoils, whatever the cause, whether the damage is serious or slight, if you're guilty or not. A fire or an explosion can be a much more destructive accident, even tragic, but it's not disgraceful, like a gelatinization. The spoiled batch contains a mocking quality: a gesture of scorn, the derisiveness of soul-less things that ought to obey you and instead rise up, defying your prudence and foresight. The unique "molecule," deformed but gigantic, that is born and dies in your hands is an obscene message and symbol: a symbol of other ugly things without reversal or remedy that obscure our future, of the prevalence of confusion over order, and of unseemly death over life.

A Tranquil Star

Once upon a time, somewhere in the universe very far away from here, lived a tranquil star, which moved tranquilly in the immensity of the sky, surrounded by a crowd of tranquil planets about which we have not a thing to report. This star was very big and very hot, and its weight was enormous: and here a reporter's difficulties begin. We have written "very far," "big," "hot," "enormous": Australia is very far, an elephant is big and a house is bigger, this morning I had a hot bath, Everest is enormous. It's clear that something in our lexicon isn't working.

If in fact this story must be written, we must have the courage to eliminate all adjectives that tend to excite wonder: they would achieve the opposite effect, that of impoverishing the narrative. For a discussion of stars our language is inadequate and seems laughable, as if someone were trying to plow with a feather. It's a language that was born with us, suitable for describing objects more or less as large and long-lasting as we are; it has our dimensions, it's human. It doesn't go beyond what our senses tell us. Until two or three hundred years ago, small meant the scabies mite; there was nothing smaller, nor, as a result, was there an adjective to describe it. The sea and the sky were big, in fact equally big; fire was hot. Not until the thirteenth century was the need felt to introduce into daily language a term suitable for counting "very" numerous objects, and, with little imagination, "million" was coined; a little later, with even less imagination, "billion" was coined, with no care being taken to give it a precise meaning, since the term today has different values in different countries.

Not even with superlatives does one get very far: how many times higher than a high tower is a very high tower? Nor can we hope for help from disguised superlatives, like "immense," "colossal," "extraordinary": to relate the things that we want to relate here, these adjectives are hopelessly unsuitable, because the star we started from was ten times as big as our sun, and the sun is "many" times as big and heavy as our Earth, whose size so overwhelms our own dimensions that we can represent it only with a violent effort of the imagination. There is, of course, the slim and elegant language of numbers, the alphabet of the powers of ten: but then this would not be a story in the sense in which this story wants to be a story; that is, a fable that awakens echoes, and in which each of us can perceive distant reflections of himself and of the human race.

This tranquil star wasn't supposed to be so tranquil. Maybe it was too big: in the far-off original act in which everything was created, it had received an inheritance too demanding. Or maybe it contained in its heart an imbalance or an infection, as happens to some of us. It's customary among the stars to quietly burn the hydrogen they are made of, generously giving energy to the void, until they are reduced to a dignified thinness and end their career as modest white dwarves. The star in question, however, when some billions of years had passed since its birth, and its companions began to rarefy, was not satisfied with its destiny and became restless: to such a point that its restlessness became visible even to those of us who are "very" distant and circumscribed by a "very" brief life.

Of this restlessness Arab and Chinese astronomers were aware. The Europeans no: the Europeans of that time, which was a time of struggle, were so convinced that the heaven of the stars was immutable, was in fact the paradigm and kingdom of immutability, that they considered it pointless and blasphemous to notice changes in it: there could be none, by definition there were none. But a diligent Arab observer, equipped only with good eyes, patience, humility, and the love of knowing the works of his God, had realized that this star, to which he was very attached, was not immutable. He had watched it for thirty years, and had noticed that the star oscillated between the 4th and the 6th of the six magnitudes that had been described many centuries earlier by a Greek, who was as diligent as he, and who, like him, thought that observing the stars was a route that would take one far. The Arab felt a little as if it were his star: he had wanted to place his mark on it, and in his notes he had called it Al-Ludra, which in his dialect means "the capricious one." Al-Ludra oscillated, but not regularly: not like a pendulum; rather, like someone who is at a loss between two choices. It completed its cycle sometimes in one year, sometimes in two, sometimes in five, and it didn't always stop in its dimming at the 6th magnitude, which is the last visible to the naked eye: at times it disappeared completely. The patient Arab counted seven cycles before he died: his life had been long, but the life of a man is always pitifully brief compared with that of a star, even if the star behaves in such a way as to arouse suspicions of its eternity.

After the death of the Arab, Al-Ludra, although provided with a name, did not attract much interest, because the variable stars are so many, and also because, starting in 1750, it was reduced to a speck, barely visible with the best telescopes of the time. But in 1950 (and the message has only now reached us) the illness that must have been gnawing at it from within reached a crisis, and here, for the second time, our story, too, enters a crisis: now it is no longer the adjectives that fail but the facts themselves. We still don't know much about the convulsive death–resurrection of stars: we know that, fairly often, something flares up in the atomic mechanism of a star's nucleus and then the star explodes, on a scale not of millions or billions of years but of hours and minutes; we know that these events are among the most cataclysmic that the sky today holds; but we understand only—and approximately—the how, not the why. We'll be satisfied with the how.

The observer who, to his misfortune, found himself on October 19th of that year, at ten o'clock our time, on one of the silent planets of Al-Ludra would have seen, "before his very eyes," as they say, his gentle sun swell, not a little but "a lot," and would not have been present at the spectacle for long. Within a quarter of an hour he would have been forced to seek useless shelter against the intolerable heat—and this we can affirm independently of any hypothesis concerning the size and shape of this observer, provided he was constructed, like us, of molecules and atoms—and in half an hour his testimony, and that of all his fellow-beings, would end. Therefore, to conclude this account, we must base it on other testimony, that of our earthly instruments, for which the event, in its intrinsic horror, happened in a "very" diluted form, besides being slowed down by the long journey through the realm of light that brought us the news. After an hour, the seas and ice (if there were any) of the no longer silent planet boiled up; after three, all its rocks melted, and its mountains crumbled into valleys in the form of lava. After ten hours, the entire planet was reduced to vapor, along with all the delicate and subtle works that the combined labor of chance and necessity, through innumerable trials and errors, had perhaps created there, and along with all the poets and wise men who had perhaps examined that sky, and had wondered what was the value of so many little lights, and had found no answer. That was the answer.

After one of our days, the surface of the star had reached the orbit of its most distant planets, invading their sky and, together with the remains of its tranquility, spreading in all directions—a billowing wave of energy bearing the modulated news of the catastrophe.

RAMÓN ESCOJIDO was thirty-four and had two charming children. With his wife he had a complex and tense relationship: he was Peruvian and she was of Austrian origin, he solitary, modest, and lazy, she ambitious and eager for social life. But what social life can you dream of if you live in an observatory at an altitude of 2900 meters, an hour's flight from the nearest city and four kilometers from an Indian village, dusty in summer and icy in winter? Judith loved and hated her husband, on alternate days, sometimes even in the same instant. She hated his wisdom and his collection of shells; she loved the father of her children, and the man who was under the covers in the morning.

They reached a fragile accord on weekend outings. It was Friday evening, and they were getting ready with noisy delight for the next day's excursion. Judith and the children were busy with the provisions; Ramón went up to the observatory to arrange the photographic plates for the night. In the morning he struggled to free himself from the children, who overwhelmed him with lighthearted questions: How far was the lake? Would it still be frozen? Had he remembered the rubber raft? He went into the darkroom to develop the plate, he dried it and placed it beside the identical plate that he had made seven days earlier. He examined both under the microscope: good, they were identical; he could leave in tranquility. But then he had a scruple and looked more carefully, and realized that there was something new; not a big thing, a barely perceptible spot, but it wasn't there on the old plate. When these things happen, ninety-nine times out of a hundred it's a speck of dust (one can never be too clean while working) or a microscopic defect in the emulsion; but there is also the minuscule probability that it's a nova, and one has to make a report, subject to confirmation. Farewell, outing: he would have to retake the photograph on the following two nights. What would he tell Judith and the children?

Dates of Original
Italian Publication

PART I: EARLY STORIES

The Death of Marinese (*Il Ponte*, August–September 1949)

Bear Meat (*Il Mondo*, August 29, 1961)

Censorship in Bitinia (*Il Mondo*, January 10, 1961)

Knall (1968–70; in Vizio di Forma, 1971)

In the Park (1968–70; in Vizio di Forma, 1971)

PART II: LATER STORIES

The Magic Paint (Tantalio; *Il Mondo*, December 27, 1973)

The Gladiators (*L'Automobile*, June 15, 1976)

The Fugitive (*La Stampa*, July 6, 1979)

One Night (*Tuttolibri*, V, no. 48–49, December 22, 1979)

Fra Diavolo on the Po (*La Stampa*, December 14, 1986)

The Sorcerers (c. 1977–78; *Lilit e altri racconti*, 1981)

Bureau of Vital Statistics (*La Stampa*, June 21, 1981)

The Girl in the Book (*La Stampa*, August 15, 1980)

Buffet Dinner (*La Stampa*, January 22, 1977)

The TV Fans from Delta Cep. (*L'Astronomia*, no. 54, April 1986)

The Molecule's Defiance (*La Stampa*, January 20, 1980)

A Tranquil Star (*La Stampa*, January 29, 1978; then in *L'Astronomia*, no. 3, March–April 1978)

ABOUT THE TRANSLATORS

ANN GOLDSTEIN has translated works by, among others, Roberto Calasso, Alessandro Baricco, Pier Paolo Pasolini, and Elena Ferrante. She has been the recipient of the PEN Renato Poggioli Award for Italian translation.

ALESSANDRA BASTAGLI is the translator from the German of Jurek Becker's *The Boxer*. She works as a book editor in New York.

JENNY MCPHEE is the author of the novels *No Ordinary Matter* and *The Center of Things*. She is the translator of Paolo Maurensig's *Canone Inverso* and *Crossing the Threshold of Hope* by Pope John Paul II.

PENGUIN MODERN CLASSICS

DANGLING MAN
SAUL BELLOW

With an Introduction by Salman Rushdie

'No contemporary writer sees more clearly than Bellow' *The Times*

Expecting to be drafted into the army during the Second World War, Joseph has given up his job and carefully prepared for his departure to the battlefront. When a series of mix-ups delays his induction, he finds himself facing a year of idleness.

Dangling Man is his journal, a wonderful account of his restless wanderings through Chicago's streets, his musings on the past, his psychological reaction to his inactivity while war rages around him, and his uneasy insights into the nature of freedom and choice.

'One of the most honest pieces of testimony on the psychology of a whole generation who have grown up during the Depression and the war' *New Yorker*

WINNER OF THE NOBEL PRIZE FOR LITERATURE

PENGUIN MODERN CLASSICS

LIFE WITH A STAR
JIRÍ WEIL

'One of the most powerful works to emerge from the Holocaust ... a fierce and necessary work of art' *The New York Times*

Prague has been occupied by the Nazis, and for Josef Roubicek, an ordinary bank clerk, life will never be the same. He is forced to wear the star of David, and overnight his world becomes alien and macabre. Disorientated, stalked by hunger, poverty and loneliness, dreaming of Ruzena, another man's wife, he roams the city. Moving and disturbing, *Life With a Star* is a compelling portrait of a man's attempt to hold on to his humanity at all costs.

'Without a doubt, one of the outstanding novels I've read about the fate of a Jew under the Nazis. I don't know of another like it' Philip Roth

With a Preface by Philip Roth
Translated by Rita Klímová with Roslyn Schloss

PENGUIN MODERN CLASSICS

THE GARDEN OF THE FINZI-CONTINIS
GIORGIO BASSANI

A new translation by Jamie McKendrick

'One of the great novelists of the last century' *Guardian*

Aristocratic, rich and seemingly aloof, the Finzi-Contini family fascinate the narrator of this tale, a young Jew in the Italian city of Ferrara. But it is not until he is a student in 1938, when anti-Semitic legislation is enforced on the eve of the Second World War, that he is invited into their luxurious estate.

As their gardens become a haven for persecuted Jews, the narrator becomes entwined in the lives of the family, and particularly close to Micòl, their daughter. Many years after the war has ended, he reflects on his memories of the Finzi-Continis, his experiences of love and loss and the fate of the family and community in the horrors of war.

PENGUIN MODERN CLASSICS

WARTIME LIES
LOUIS BEGLEY

With an Afterword by Louis Begley

'A remarkable, elegiac novel' *Time*

As the world slips into the throes of the Second World War, young Maciek is about to see his warm and protected childhood vanish forever – for he is a Jew living in south-east Poland. Maciek and his beautiful, acerbic and brave Aunt Tania, always together, constantly on the run, using forged identity papers and names that are not their own, manage to stay just ahead of Germans bent on the extermination of Polish Jews.

Gripping and intensely moving, *Wartime Lies* is a story of high courage and adventure that looks unblinkingly at the cost of survival.

Winner of the *Irish Times* International Fiction Prize and of the PEN/Ernest Hemingway Foundation Award for a First Work of Fiction and the French Prix Médicis Etranger

PENGUIN MODERN CLASSICS

THE SEARCH FOR ROOTS
PRIMO LEVI

'A dark, disturbing, bright and uplifting book' *The Times*

The Search for Roots is an anthology of writings that Primo Levi considered to be essential reading. Fiction, poetry, science, philosophy and travellers' tales are to be found among these thirty pieces, each with an introduction by Levi. He presents familiar voices – Swift, Conrad, T. S. Eliot and Arthur C. Clarke – and introduces us to less familiar ones: Lucretius, Giuseppe Belli, Fredric Brown and Hermann Langbein. All reflect Levi's deep passion for literature, his profound knowledge of science, and his survival of Auschwitz, making it a collection that is both universal and poignantly autobiographical.

'A book packed with pleasurable reading, value and, crucially, with profound insight into this most essential of writers' Robert S. C. Gordon, *Spectator*

'*The Search for Roots* … is Primo Levi's best autobiography' Carole Angier, *New Statesman*

Translated with an Introduction by Peter Forbes

With an Afterword by Italo Calvino

PENGUIN MODERN CLASSICS

MOMENTS OF REPRIEVE
PRIMO LEVI

'One of the most important and gifted writers of our time' Italo Calvino

Primo Levi was one of the most astonishing voices to emerge from the twentieth century: a man who survived one of the ugliest times in history, yet who was able to describe his own Auschwitz experience with an unaffected tenderness.

Levi was a master storyteller but he did not write fairytales. These stories are an elegy to the human figures who stood out against the tragic background of Auschwitz, 'the ones in whom I had recognised the will and capacity to react, and hence a rudiment of virtue'. Each centres on an individual who – whether it be through a juggling trick, a slice of apple or a letter – discovers one of the 'bizarre, marginal moments of reprieve'.

Translated by Ruth Feldman

With an Introduction by Michael Ignatieff

*Contemporary ... Provocative ... Outrageous ...
Prophetic ... Groundbreaking ... Funny ... Disturbing ...
Different ... Moving ... Revolutionary ... Inspiring ...
Subversive ... Life-changing ...*

What makes a modern classic?

At Penguin Classics our mission has always been to make the best
books ever written available to everyone. And that also means
constantly redefining and refreshing exactly what makes a 'classic'.
That's where Modern Classics come in. Since 1961 they have been an
organic, ever-growing and ever-evolving list of books from the last
hundred (or so) years that we believe will continue to be read over and
over again.

They could be books that have inspired political dissent, such as
Animal Farm. Some, like *Lolita* or *A Clockwork Orange*, may have
caused shock and outrage. Many have led to great films, from *In Cold
Blood* to *One Flew Over the Cuckoo's Nest*. They have broken down
barriers – whether social, sexual, or, in the case of *Ulysses*, the
boundaries of language itself. And they might – like *Goldfinger* or
Scoop – just be pure classic escapism. Whatever the reason, Penguin
Modern Classics continue to inspire, entertain and enlighten millions
of readers everywhere.

'No publisher has had more influence on reading habits than Penguin'
Independent

'Penguins provided a crash course in world literature'
Guardian

The best books ever written

PENGUIN 🐧 CLASSICS

SINCE 1946

Find out more at www.penguinclassics.com